春秋時代之國際制度

吳克著

李田意題

This volume is the first of a number in which it is planned to publish the results of research carried on by faculty and research scholars working at Yale University in the field of Foreign Area Studies. Subsequent volumes will include studies in the various disciplines, both Humanities and Social Sciences; in respect to East Asia, Southeast Asia and the Soviet Union. The undersigned are acting as general editors for the purpose of securing and approving the best possible results of research in these fields at Yale. In the various disciplines or areas to which the special skills of this committee group do not directly apply, it is planned to secure supplementary advice from both inside and outside the University. In this way it is hoped that in the next several years a number of studies now completed, or which are in an advanced state of development, may be made available to the scholarly world.

David Nelson Rowe,
 Chairman, Editorial Committee
 Professor of Political Science
William S. Cornyn,
 Associate Professor of
 Burmese and Slavic Languages
Karl J. Pelzer,
 Professor of Geography

Yale University
October 1953

THE MULTI-STATE SYSTEM

OF

ANCIENT CHINA

by

Richard Louis Walker

**Assistant Professor of History
and Fellow of Trumbull College
in Yale University**

The Shoe String Press ·   Hamden 17, Connecticut

This book is humbly dedicated to

CHARLES SIDNEY GARDNER

to whose unselfish assistance

American scholarship on China owes a timeless debt

TABLE OF CONTENTS

PREFACE

The Chinese have usually maintained that the lessons
for any generation are available from the past. Historians
of all cultures have ever been fascinated by the astonish-
ing parallels which they discover between the present and
former times. Yet these historians have also been the
first to point out the danger of pursuing parallels too
closely.

Perhaps the hardest task in writing this volume has
been that of resisting the temptation to draw the many
parallels which are so obvious. In some cases similari-
ties between the experiences in China during the Spring
and Autumn Period and events at later times in the West
are unbelievably precise. There is, for example, the temptation to compare the position of the Chou king with that
of the Pope in the sixteenth or seventeenth century in
Europe; the role of ceremony with the diplomatic proto-
col of the court of Louis XIV; the Chin alliance with Wu
with the alliance between Francis I and the Ottoman
Turks; or the leagues of states with NATO and other
recent collective security arrangements. Such compari-
sons, however, have a double danger. They set the mind
of the Western reader to thinking along conventional lines,
carrying along overtones which do not conform with the
facts. Likewise they prevent the portrayal of the ancient
Chinese sovereign state system as the unique and isolated
case which it certainly was.

This study has a specialized and limited objective--
the political analysis of a system of sovereign states. It
is therefore not to be construed as a social or economic
history, nor a political history in the strict sense of the
term. Yet it is hoped that in a small way it will constitute
a contribution to an understanding of a very important
period in Chinese history. It was, in different form, the
author's doctoral dissertation presented to Yale University
in 1950.

The volume is intended primarily for two scholarly
interest groups. To one group, the sinologists, much of

the material is well known. Perhaps they will find some few new data in this interpretation which supports the recent critical Chinese scholarship on the historical period involved. They may also find some small help in the footnote references which are primarily intended for their use. For the other group, the modern international relations specialists, I feel sure that the material will prove new, and I can only hope interesting and valuable.

It is impossible to list all of the people who have helped me in my work on this volume, but a few deserve special mention. David N. Rowe contributed untold hours of editing, and his many suggestions were of inspiration and great value. Charles S. Gardner's careful notes have saved me from numerous blunders. George A. Kennedy, Yang Lien-sheng, and Edwin O. Reischauer have also given valuable time to read the manuscript, as has a very dear friend Li T'ien-yi, whose calligraphy graces the title page. I am likewise grateful to Charles Chu, Dorothy and Toshio Kono and Irma Lathrop for their help with the manuscript. To Arthur W. Hummel and Wang En-pao of the Library of Congress and to the staff of the Yale University Library I owe great thanks for invaluable assistance. Only many sacrifices and long hours devoted by my wife, Celeno, however, have made it possible for me to acknowledge the assistance of these other friends.

Richard L. Walker

Morningside
Milford, Connecticut
August 1953

THE MULTI-STATE SYSTEM
OF
ANCIENT CHINA

Chapter I

MULTI-STATE SYSTEMS

The simple fact of conflict among politically organized groups--war--has occasioned more thought, study and fruitless hopes than any other item in the chronicles of mankind. Few have questioned the desirability of eliminating war, many have proposed schemes to that end, but no one has succeeded in providing an answer to the problem. Wars continue to plague humanity; and the plague grows in intensity because, while few improvements have been made in the means for preventing armed conflict, the capabilities for mass destruction have reached their ultimate form in weapons which can destroy the world.

Approaches to the problem of war have varied through the ages. Philosophers and prophets have offered solutions in terms of ideal political organizations or new moral codes. These solutions have in turn been tested by ardent disciples who have shortly after their failure either abandoned them or else blamed others rather than re-examine the doctrines of their teachers. Thus those who followed Karl Marx and saw the origins of conflict in the struggles of economically determined classes have either forsaken his narrow basis of analysis or have in turn carried it to the point where they are themselves generating conflicts which they blame on those who will not accept the dictates of their doctrine. Disciples of other prophets cling to the hope that the true teachings of their masters will someday be adopted by a wholly rational or fully enlightened humanity. Thus, for example, Carl J. Friedrich sees in the categorical imperative of Immanuel Kant the certainty of 'Inevitable Peace.'[1] But unfortunately the conflicts of today threaten the extinction of rational beings before Kant's epitome of rationalism can be realized by all humanity.

The twentieth century students of international relations have shown at least as much versatility in their approach to the problem of war as the philosophers and prophets of the past. In the early years of the century a prevailing optimism led many to the conclusion that peace could shortly be attained through the spread of democracy and international understanding and through the proliferation of the methods of arbitration.[2] The disillusionment following World War I caused some to search for 'the' person or persons responsible for war and others to seek 'the' cause or causes. The former optimism prevailed among many who believed that if 'the' cause could be discovered, it could be dealt with and peace could be assured for the future. The devil theory of war was one of the characteristic interpretations during the inter-war period. Congressional investigators in the United States searched into the activities of munitions makers and the scholars drew some hope from their findings.[3]

World War II offered convincing proof to the many peace foundations, research groups, and individual scholars, that their work had hardly begun and, indeed, that much of it had been based upon assumptions which were at least open to question. Optimism has, however, continued. One present group sees in the expanded services of the new collective security structure, the United Nations, the answer to the problem. Another has decided that world government offers the only hope for peace but is unable to say how unwilling sovereign powers are going to be enlisted without causing the war they seek to prevent. Another world-wide effort, UNESCO, is placing great faith in the creation of international understanding with the conviction expressed in its constitution that "since wars begin in the minds of men, it is in the minds of men that the defenses of peace must be constructed."[4]

Inevitably analysis of the problem of conflict must turn to the experiences of the past. Here the historians have pointed out that the origins of war are so complex that the human mind is incapable of complete understanding. The shifting weights of the various factors behind each case of organized violence make it unique. This does not mean that attempts to eliminate war are doomed to failure from the start. But it does mean that there cannot be a single, simple overall solution. Today's scholars have apparently at long last abandoned the single-factor approach which, though attractive, has proved so illusory.

No longer do they start with such questions as, "Is it man's basic nature?" or, "What is wrong with our institutions?"

The present trend is to utilize recent developments in such fields as psychology and anthropology to supplement historical analysis.[5] There is a recognition that theories must be stated in relative terms and that all of them are at best only partial answers to the problem. Hypotheses regarding war are now usually stated as a series of expectations--under such-and-such conditions war is more (or less) likely to occur. They recognize that their hypotheses must still be supported by an exhaustive examination of historical experience.

One factor important in past conflicts and on which a series of hypotheses would prove most valuable is the political framework within which the most violent conflicts have been generated--the sovereign or multi-state system. Whenever conflict between organized groups occurs, some question of sovereignty is involved. Thus the existence of any system within which the individual groups insist on sovereign rights is worthy of study as a prototype of the modern world-embracing sovereign state system. It is desirable to know under what conditions the simple existence of such a system can in itself tend to promote organized violence. What limits does it set on actions designed to eliminate conflict? Under what conditions does the existence of a system of sovereign states tend to discourage conflict?

It is probable then that a very fruitful path in dealing with the problem of war lies in the examination of multi-state systems as such. Yet, for all their versatility, the modern scholars have not followed this path to any great extent. Undoubtedly a major reason is because it is difficult to view the present system of sovereign states in this manner. For, since it embraces the whole world, analysis must perforce be made from within the system. There have, however, been other cases of multi-state systems within the recorded history of mankind; and some of these have been almost as clearly delimited as ours today. An analysis of these systems can offer us data for support of hypotheses as to when and under what conditions we may expect the existence of a system of sovereign states to operate in the direction of creating or alleviating war.

Some analyses of other multi-state systems have

already been made. The relations among the states of
Ancient Greece have been the subject of several studies.[6]
Machiavelli made penetrating observations on state be-
havior within the city-state system of Renaissance Italy.
Narendra Law has offered a short study of Interstate Re-
lations in Ancient India,[7] based for the most part on the
Kautiliya, an old Indian political treatise.

Another system of sovereign states existed in China
before the dawn of the Christian era. It offers at least
two major advantages as a type study of multi-state
systems. In the first place, this system existed in a
nearly perfect state of isolation. It constituted almost as
closed an arena as the world today. Secondly, China, like
India, is an area of cultural experience vastly different
from the West. Therefore any confirmations of previous
generalizations and expectations about multi-state systems
or the behavior of states within them will be of great value.
Data contrary to former conclusions will offer bases for
reexamination of the hypotheses which led to those conclusions.

Fortunately this period of Chinese history has been
extensively studied, and most of the sources and documents have been evaluated. There are, to be sure, facts
which we can never know, and there are still many objects
to be unearthed--but the broad outlines of the working of
the multi-state system are sufficiently clear to allow
objective analysis. On many of the details there is a
surprising wealth of material.

The presentation of the data on Ancient China in the
form of an analysis of a system of sovereign states involves
an approach to Chinese history which is certainly not traditional. It is perhaps best, then, to turn to some of the
historical background before examining the operation of
the multi-state system.

to overthrow the ancient system of traditions
and cults.

Once we have passed the crucial date of 200
B. C. , however, conditions are radically
changed. The system of feudal kingdoms that
had flourished for a millennium had entirely
broken down.

It is only in the past few decades that careful research and modern criticism have enabled the partial
penetration of the Han gloss. This has for the most part
been done by a group of Chinese scholars who have
broken away from the Confucian tradition and have
approached their national history with the tools of various specialized disciplines developed in the West. They
have been asking questions about their past which the
power of orthodoxy prevented former generations of Chinese scholars from daring to raise. Likewise the work
of the Japanese students of Chinese history in reexamining the early periods has been prodigious. Unfortunately,
most of the modern Western historians of China have not
kept up with these new developments and are still pictur-
ing the history of pre-Han China in Han terms.[10]
Foremost among the Chinese historians who have been
reexamining their past is Professor Ku Chieh-kang 顧
頡剛 . He started where the grand old scholar Wang
Kuo-wei 王國維 left off, and the volumes of the Ku Shih
Pien 古史辨 Ancient History Disputes which he has edited
and published, must hereafter form a starting point for
those who wish to study China before Ch'in times. The
proof which he and his fellow scholars have mustered for
a different interpretation of early Chinese history is
extremely convincing. They have demonstrated that the
supposed unity under the Chou and earlier dynasties is
little more than a myth, and they have reexamined the
ancient works with that fact in mind.[11]
Other modern Chinese scholars have studied the pre-
Ch'in history from still different points of view.
Professor Li Hsüan-po 李玄伯 , a trained sociologist and
anthropologist, inspired by Durkheim and Fustel de
Coulanges, published his First Draft of New Researches
in Ancient Chinese Society in 1941. In it for the first time
he compared ancient Chinese society with modern primitive

societies and drew some rather original conclusions about
such topics as family, state, king, totemic society and political centralization, in Ancient China.[12]

Undoubtedly the most drastic break with past
scholarly tradition in the study of Ancient China was
made by those scholars who worked in the prevailing
climate of Marxism which pervaded Chinese learned
circles in the 1930's. They concentrated their attention
on the economic side of Chou life and especially on means
of production and changing economic patterns. The influence of Marxism is present in the pages of the Ku Shih
Pien, and two other journals which contain valuable contributions to the study of the Chou period--Shih Huo
食貨 Food and Commodities and Yü Kung 禹貢 Tribute of
Yü--were published largely under Marxist auspices.[13]
Among the Chinese Marxists several are important,
despite methodological limitations, for the study of Ch'un-
ch'iu social and economic life: Kuo Mo-jo 郭沫若 , the
present 'Cultural Commissar' of Communist China,
has followed the Stalinist line abjectly in applying Marx's
nineteenth century terminology to ancient Chinese economic life; T'ao Hsi-sheng 陶希聖 has made several penetrating observations on Chou society, but is also handi-
capped by the limited Marxist jargon; Hou Wai-lu 侯外廬
is even more doctrinnaire, but his work cannot be
ignored; Chi Chao-ting 冀朝鼎 represents an unorthodox
offshoot, largely influenced by K. A. Wittfogel, and has
made important contributions to an understanding of the
role played by water control in "key economic areas" in
a reciprocal influence on social and political institutions.
Unfortunately the Marxist influence since the 1930's has
been sufficiently strong in studies of the Chou period to
limit the amount of ethnological and anthropological research in China. This has for the most part been done in
Japan and in the West.[14]

Still other difficulties have faced those modern students who have tried to understand pre-Ch'in China. In
addition to the fact that tradition probably means more to
the Chinese than to any other people-- and Han history is
a strong part of their tradition--there is the fact
mentioned above that most of the important records and
books were burned in 213 B. C. under the orders of Ch'in
Shih Huang.[15] There is yet another important reason why
the actualities of the Chou period have not been discovered

until recent times. It was the Eastern Chou period which
produced those philosophers and thinkers who were to
have the most important influence upon the course of
Chinese civilization. It is quite possible that the imprint
of their doctrines upon Chinese culture under the Han
dynasty was more important than the actual course of political events in the period in which they themselves lived.
Confucius, Mencius, Hsün-tzu, Mo Ti, Lao-tzu, Chuang-
tzu--it is quite understandable that later Chinese historians should be more concerned with the lives and thoughts
of these men than with the society in which they lived and
which they characterized as one of immoral and unnatural
strife.[16] This concern of the traditional Chinese historians has carried over to the Western histories of China
in which the Eastern Chou period is frequently characterized by some such title as 'The Age of the Philosophers.'

This is not to say that the philosophers of the
Eastern Chou period were unimportant in their time,
though they were far more important later, for the imprint left by their fictionalized accounts of antiquity. But
the preoccupation with the philosophers has tended to
obscure the actual development of Chinese political institutions in pre-Ch'in times. Then, too, this preoccupation
was concerned merely with those philosophers whose
ideas survived the book-burning. The works of other
philosophers--especially political theorists with perhaps
a more realistic interpretation of the age--had disappeared forever. The truth is that in order to appreciate
and understand the philosophies which originated in the
Eastern Chou period, we need a much clearer picture of
that period in its totality.

All this is background necessary for an understanding of why the political life of the Eastern Chou has not
until recently been studied as a system of sovereign
states. A period in which over 170 small states are con-
solidated into less than a score of large and ambitious
ones is obviously a period of important political
change.[17] Such a period of significant political experience
deserves careful study. One of the results of the new
approach to Chinese history in this ancient period has
been to emphasize the need for such study. It is entirely
possible, for example, that the serious nature of the
changes which he was witnessing is what prompted

Confucius to edit the annals of his state and to tell his
disciples "It is the 'Spring and Autumn' which will make
men know me, and it is the 'Spring and Autumn' which
will make men condemn me."[18]

Two commentaries on the Annals became extremely
popular among the scholars of the Former Han dynasty,
the Kung Yang 公羊 commentary sponsored by Tung
Chung-shu 董仲舒 and the Ku Liang 穀梁 commentary
supported by Liu Hsiang 劉向. These commentaries
represent the "praise and blame" schools which interpret
the entries of Confucius as attempts to pass moral judg-
ments upon the actions recorded--judgments based upon
a presumed Chou unity and superiority. In addition, the
Kung Yang commentary provided the Han rulers with the
convenient theory of the 'Mandate of Heaven' which was
to become an important factor in Chinese political history through succeeding centuries.[19] Possibly in order to
fit the Annals into his conception of one empire which he
felt to be the only answer to the problem of peace in his
time, Confucius did change some of the titles (cheng ming
正名) to establish a pat feudal heirarchy--but the events
recorded belie any overall unity for China in the Spring
and Autumn Period. Indeed, in the very first entries of
the Annals, we find one of the states, Cheng 鄭 , making
an attack upon the domain of the Chou king.

The Tso-chuan 左傳 or Commentary of Tso upon the
annals, on the other hand, presents for the most part an
elaboration of the events recorded--the stories are well
told, and the facts are quite reliable. Its 170,000 Chinese
words--at least double that many in English translation--
constitute "perhaps our most important single source on
Chou dynasty China."[20] There has been a great amount
of work done by competent scholars on the authenticity of
the Tso-chuan and its place among the source materials
on Ancient China. They have convincingly refuted the
position of the nineteenth century Chinese scholar K'ang
Yu-wei 康有為 that the text had been greatly tampered
with and forged in part by Liu Hsin 劉歆 and have established its position as a reliable pre-Ch'in record.[21]

Thus, the Tso-chuan, and the work usually closely
associated with it, the Kuo-yü 國語 or Discourses of the
States, are of necessity the main foundation for any study
of the Ch'un-ch'iu period. The present study is no
exception. There are, of course, other works which date

back to Ancient China. The annals of the State of Ch'in
have been preserved in the Shih-chi 史記 of Ssu-ma
Ch'ien 司馬遷 , [22] but they are much more spotty; and we
cannot know how much Ssu-ma tampered with them. There
are also the Bamboo Annals or Chu-shu Chi-nien 竹書紀年
which are supposedly the records of the Wei court. These
are even more fragmentary than those of Ch'in. [23] Both
have little value for our study except to confirm the dates
of the main events.

Other writings are attributed to the pre-Ch'in period,
but their use presents formidable difficulties. Since most
of them have been preserved through Han editing, it
becomes difficult to distinguish those which are authentic
from those which are not genuine early texts. Some
modern scholars such as Lou Kan-jou, in order to be on
absolutely certain ground, restrict themselves to the
Ch'un-ch'iu, Tso-chuan, and Kuo-yü only, and rely on
inscriptions and archeological findings for supplementary
data. [24] Professor Bernhard Karlgren has recently suggested a classification system which would distinguish
between what he calls 'free' or pre-Han texts and the
'systematizing' Han texts. He then divides the latter into
Early Han and Late Han. His study of legends and cults
in Ancient China has convinced him that the later Han
scholars applied an even more rigid imaginative gloss to
antiquity than did the early Han scholars. [25] This, of
course, places a premium on the accurate classification
of early texts. Fortunately a great amount of work has
already been done in that field. In our study of the workings of the multi-state system of Ancient China we shall
limit ourselves as much as possible to the 'free' texts
and, of course, to the work of the modern scholars who
take into account the recent work done on bronze and
bone inscriptions and other archeological findings.

This leads to an acceptance of the view of Ku Chieh-
kang and his associates that most of the concept of Chou
Empire, as we have hitherto known it, is a creation of the
philosophers and the Han historical imagination. In other
words, there probably never was much of a Chou empire
to break to pieces. [26] Thus the approach to the political
analysis of the Ch'un-ch'iu period followed here accents
changes and innovations rather than the uniformities of
the system. The stress will be on dynamics. We shall be
interested in the changes in political structure within the

individual states, the emergence of new groups as chal-
lengers for political power, the development of new
methods for handling the relations among the many sovereign states, and, to a certain extent, changes in the
economic and social structure. [27]

One technique which is of value in this type of
analysis has already been used with great effectiveness
by Professor George A. Kennedy for a study of the Ch'un-
ch'iu. He divides the Ch'un-ch'iu into twelve periods of
twenty years each. [28] An analysis of the records of the
deaths of rulers in each period has enabled him not only
to eliminate once and for all the possibility of reading a
cryptographic morality into the chronicle but also
to indicate in rough form the expanding area of contact among the various states. His work is the first to
subject the Confucian chronicle to this type of trend
analysis, and the results which he has achieved bear out
some of the conclusions which the authors of the Ku Shih
Pien have reached by different methods. In the analysis
to follow we shall use this same method of dividing the
Ch'un-ch'iu into twelve twenty-year periods in order to
chart some of the important trends in the political and
economic fields. The following table indicates the twelve
periods hereafter identified by the Roman numerals
assigned to them:

Period	Years	Reign Years of Dukes of Lu				
I	720-701	Yin 隱	3	-	Huan 桓	11
II	700-681	Huan 桓	12	-	Chuang 莊	13
III	680-661	Chuang 莊	14	-	Min 閔	1
IV	660-641	Min 閔	2	-	Hsi 僖	19
V	640-621	Hsi 僖	20	-	Wen 文	6
VI	620-601	Wen 文	7	-	Hsüan 宣	8
VII	600-581	Hsüan 宣	9	-	Ch'eng 成	10
VIII	580-561	Ch'eng 成	11	-	Hsiang 襄	12
IX	560-541	Hsiang 襄	13	-	Chao 昭	1
X	540-521	Chao 昭	2	-	Chao 昭	21
XI	520-501	Chao 昭	22	-	Ting 定	9
XII	500-481	Ting 定	10	-	Ai 哀	4

Before turning to the workings of the multi-state
system, it is probably desirable to mention briefly some
of the social and economic background of the Ch'un-ch'iu
period. Here also, as we shall see in the political field,

the period is marked by constant development and great change. According to one modern Chinese historian, "The Ch'un-ch'iu Chan-kuo period was the most severe era of transformation in the history of Chinese social organization."[29] The Ch'un-ch'iu is a period of constantly widening horizons and of steady growth in the ease of communications. On this score the chronicle itself presents an admirably clear picture without the aid of the commentary. Professor Kennedy's tables indicate the ever increasing scope of diplomatic activity at Lu on the basis of the reports of deaths of rulers of different states which were brought in person by the emissaries of those states. [30] Mei Ssu-p'ing also notes this same fact. He divides the Ch'un-ch'iu into three sub-divisions, roughly embracing periods I-IV, V-IX, and X-XII. He then notes that in the first sub-division there is hardly any contact outside the area embraced by the original Chou states, but that by the middle of the third, the area of contact had expanded far to the north and south. [31]

A further indication of the increasing ease of communication can be seen in the following table. By recording the reports of peaceful diplomatic missions carried on by the state of Lu outside its borders over a period of ten years at the start of every third period--i. e. , I, IV, VII, and X--and calculating the number of miles of travel involved, we get the following:[32]

TABLE I

<u>Diplomatic Missions By Lu Outside Its Borders</u>

	PERIOD			
	I	IV	VII	X
	(720-	(660-	(600-	(540-
	701)	641)	581)	521)
Number of missions	7	8	10	15
Total mileage involved	780	1650	2580	6360
Av. Miles for each mission	112	206	258	454
Missions by the Duke	7	5	4	3
Missions by Duke's family	0	2	0	0
Missions by Officers of Lu	0	1	6	12

It is interesting to note that in every one of the seven

missions reported for the first ten years of Period I, the
Duke of Lu met the other ruler involved at a point approximately half-way between the two capitals. Three of the
eight missions reported in the first ten years of Period
IV, however, involved trips the full distance to the capital
of the other state. By Period X the Duke of Lu journeyed
the whole way to the capital of the state of Ch'u 楚 , some
525 miles straight-line distance, and in that period 12 of
the trips outside the borders of Lu involved going to the
capitals of the other states. The listing of who was involved in the mission bears out a tendency, which we shall
note below (Chapter V), for the handling of external affairs
to become more and more the function of specialized per-
sonnel. We note the fact here as a further indication of
the developing complexity and diversification in the social
life through the course of the Ch'un-ch'iu period.

The ever-increasing contacts in Ancient China aided
in augmenting trade and spreading prosperity. [33] With
this came the growth of a money economy. We know of
the existence of shell-money as far back as Shang times,
but with the Ch'un-ch'iu comes the development of coins.
Archeological findings indicate that there was far more
money in circulation than previous students had assumed. [34]
The constant use of the characters for riches, fu 富 and
kuei 貴 , in the Analects of Confucius indicates that by the
close of the Spring and Autumn times new classes were
arising based upon wealth. [35] Wealth became transport-
able. A story in the Tso-chuan for the year 545 B.C.
discusses the riches of a certain citizen of Ch'i 齊 by
name Ch'ing Feng 慶封 . Because of the life of debauch-
ery which his riches enabled him to lead, he was
eventually forced to leave his home state and go to Lu.
"By-and-by the people of Ch'i sent to reproach (Lu for
sheltering him), on which he fled to Wu, where Chü-yü
gave him Chu-fang. There he collected the members of
his clan and settled them, becoming richer than he had
ever been before." [36] Ch'ing Feng was evidently able to
transport his wealth first to Lu and then to Wu. Private
ownership increased constantly, and by the middle of the
Ch'un-ch'iu it was an obvious development in most of the
countries. [37] With increasing frequency we find mention
of the erection of new buildings and of elaborate palaces.
In 542 B.C., for example, Tso reports that Duke Hsiang
had erected a palace after the style of those in Ch'u where

he had visited two years before. [38]

Growing prosperity becomes more apparent through
the pages of the Tso-chuan, and archeological findings
have borne out Tso's reports. For example, there have
been finds of an increasing number of clothing and
carriage ornaments from the latter years of the Ch'un-
ch'iu. At that time also we find the development of
bronzes for decorating homes. [39] Many of the bronze
vessels which in Shang times had been used almost exclusively for sacrificial purposes became household
vessels in the palaces of the royal families of the various states toward the close of the Ch'un-ch'iu. [40] There
were an ever-increasing number of chariots for public
use. Members of the richer or noble families were able
to employ more and more servants and slaves. In 679
B. C. 66 slaves were killed to accompany Duke Wu of
Ch'in 秦武公 to his grave. A little over fifty years later
almost three times that number (177) accompanied Duke
Mu 穆 to his grave. [41]

Of course, the main reason for the increasing prosperity was the great improvement in the means of production
and distribution. The Spring and Autumn Period witnessed
the utilization of iron on an extensive scale, both for
weapons of war and in agriculture. The introduction of the
ox-drawn plow marked a great advance. Increasing commerce made greater specialization possible, and made
available a greater variety of products in the market-place.
The question naturally arises as to just how much it was
actually possible to transport from one place to another.
An incident related in the Tso-chuan in the year 493 B. C.,
toward the very end of the Ch'un-ch'iu, gives rather
eloquent testimony. The ruler of Ch'i was helping to
support a revolt within Chin 晋. At one point in the
struggle the leader of the rebellion was in the town of
Chao-ko 朝湄 and in dire straits. Ch'i sent a convoy of
grain to help meet his needs. The convoy was intercepted
and over 1000 wagon-loads of grain were seized. Chao-ko
was at least 300 miles from Ch'i. [42]

Undoubtedly much economic growth was fostered by
state action. One of the key activities which aided and
was in turn aided by the growth of state power was the
construction of large-scale waterworks projects for
irrigation and flood control. Such projects stemming
back to Shang times showed steady advance in the

Ch'un-ch'iu. [43] Giant dykes and canals were already
being constructed by some of the more powerful states.
Such projects made possible the increased agricultural
production which in turn freed manpower for participation
in the growing ranks of the bureaucracy. The foundations
for what Wittfogel has called the "hydraulic society" of
China with its intensive patterns of control and large body
of state functionaries were well laid during this period.
The establishment of large state monopolies of iron, salt,
liquor, etc. were also a concomitant development. [44]

The recent studies of the Chinese Marxists are the
foremost in pointing out that this did not necessarily
mean an appreciable improvement in the life of the
common man in Ancient China. They are, of course,
interested in applying the terms of the class-struggle
theory to the process which was taking place. There was,
however, an increase in the numbers at the top of the
pyramid. The Ch'un-ch'iu marks the gradual emergence
of new social and economic groupings and a rapid increase
in their numbers and relative importance within the social
structure: merchants, artisans, and especially bureaucrats,
elbowing the aristocracy for recognition. In their increasing prosperity these new groups tended to support each
other. A good example is furnished in the states of Ch'i
and Ch'u where industries became so important that
special officers, the Kung-cheng 工 正 , had to be
appointed to look after the artisans. Of particular importance in developing new classes were the rapidly
developing salt and iron industries in Ch'i and Chin. [45]
These developments on the social and economic side
coupled with changes which we shall note in the political
structure helped to do away with the most important
elements of the feudal system which had been created at
the start of Chou times.

It is important to understand the extent to which the
earlier feudalism was gradually watered down during the
Spring and Autumn Period, for it is but the reflection of
the progress being made in the political and social fields.
The usual characterization of this period of Ancient China
as a feudal period is entirely misleading--it distracts
attention from the dynamics and focuses it on rather
meaningless, if still persistent, titles and relationships. [46]

Keeping in mind the dynamic character of the period,
and with this preliminary glance at the social and economic

background, let us turn our attention first of all to the
political units which were utilizing these changes for
their increasing strength and expansion--the individual
states.

Chapter III

THE INDIVIDUAL STATES

Traditional history reports that the Chou conqueror and his successors set up 1,773 states in the area where the Chou established their power.[1] While this seems to be quite a large number, it is not impossible that the Chou leader did delegate one of his relatives or supporters to take charge of each of the many towns or settlements which he conquered. This would have made each of these towns as independent entity owing its allegiance to the Chou king under the feudal order which he had instituted.

Already by the start of the Ch'un-ch'iu period a process of consolidation had taken place. Towns pushing out their areas had come into contact and conflict, and the weaker ones were absorbed by the stronger. Some alliances were formed, but the allegiance to the Chou ruler still formed the main bulwark against the ruder tribes which roamed outside the pale of Chou civilization to the West. By 771, the individual states were sufficiently interested in their own pursuits to prevent the Chou king from organizing them to repel a barbarian attack, and, as we have seen, the capital had to be moved. By the beginning of the Lu chronicles in 722 B. C. there were only about 170 states in the area of Chou control.[2] Of these a few had already started to emerge as important: Lu 魯, Cheng 鄭, Wei 衛, Sung 宋, Chi 杞, Ch'en 陳, Ts'ao 曹, Ts'ai 蔡, Ch'i 齊, and Chou itself were the states in this area which had accumulated sufficient power to enable them to maintain their importance through most of the Ch'un-ch'iu period.

At the end of this era there were only 13 important states, and these included five which lay outside the Chou realm.[3] The implications are quite obvious. The larger Chou states had achieved their position by a process of aggression against and absorption of their weaker neighbors. Yet there were limitations to the amount of territory which they could control. They were surrounded, as we shall see, by four larger states, so that after a certain

point was reached, the only method of expansion was by
the conquest of each other. The exception was the state
of Ch'i which was able to expand its territory to the east
in the Shantung promontory. These states had the initial
advantage of a superior culture and better developed
methods of warfare, so that at the start of the Ch'un-ch'iu
they constituted the main powers. They had developed
among themselves a highly regulated and specialized
method of maintaining relations, and this was linked with
the ceremonies of the time. Thus, Chou continued to have
some weight with these states because it constituted a
ritual center. Lu's position was unique too in that it had
been founded by the famous Duke of Chou and maintained
the closest resemblance to Chou in the conduct of its
ceremonies and relations--i.e. its li 禮 . Tso states
that when a Chin envoy visited Lu in 540 B. C. and
examined the Lu archives, he exclaimed, "The institutes
(li) of Chou are all in Lu. Now, indeed, I know the virtue
of the Duke of Chou, and how it was that Chou attained to
the royal dignity."[4]

These then were the central states, the Chung-kuo
中國 (the modern name for China). At the start of the
Ch'un-ch'iu they were of approximately equal power.[5]
They maintained the feudal pattern despite their growth,
and this prevented them from developing political institutions commensurate with their size. Consequently, they
were soon outstripped in power by the states which were
better situated to expand. United, they formed a center of
power to be reckoned with; disunited, they had to bend to
the will of the more powerful states outside. Disunited
they soon were, not only because there was no strong political control by Chou, but because of their own conflict-
ing ambitions.[6]

Outside the pale of the cultural development in the
central area were the states which had more room for
expansion and which were less closely tied to the original
feudal system which had been created by the Chou. But if
the traditional historians claimed a former unity of all
these states under the Chou empire, how did they fit these
states in? Their answer was in the creation of an elaborate system of genealogies by which all of the rulers of
these outer states were related to the Chou house.[7] In
some cases it was supposed that members of the Chou
house were sent out to rule these ruder tribes, in others

the outer states were considered part of the original land
allotment. Let us, however, examine two extreme cases--
the states of Yen 燕 and Wu 吳 -- the first far to the
northeast and the second far to the southeast. Yen was
supposedly given as a fief to the son of Duke Shao by
King Wu 武 (1134 B.C.) of Chou. Wu was said to have
been founded by the uncles of King Wen 文 (1142 B.C.)
The modern scholar Ch'i Ssu-ho, utilizing inscriptions
and archeological discoveries, has demonstrated that
these are nothing but legends and poorly founded legends
at that.[8] Once these states came into contact with those
in the center they quickly recognized the superior culture,
and they did make marriage alliances, but only well after
the beginning of the Ch'un-ch'iu period.

In the upper Yellow River valley were the states of
Ch'in 秦 , Chin 晉 , Yü 虞 , Kuo 虢 and Liang 梁 embrac-
ing most of present-day Shansi and Shensi provinces. In
the Yangtze and Han River valleys were the states of
Ch'u 楚 , Sui 隨 , Shen 申 , Hsi 息 , Su 徐 , T'eng 鄧 ,
Chiao 絞 , Chow 州 , and Pa 巴 constituting most of the
present provinces of Hupei, Anhui, and eastern Szechwan.
To the southeast in the present province of Kiangsu were
the states of Wu 吳 and Yüeh 越 ; and far to the northeast
near present Peiping was the capital of the state of
Yen 燕 . These constituted the major states outside the
Chou center. Far outside on the perimeter of these states
were some wilder tribes, a few of which had fairly permanent seats of power. These barbarians were characterized by the four titles Yi 夷 , Jung 戎 , Man 蠻 , and
Ti 狄 according to the direction (east, west, south, and
north respectively) in which they were encountered. (See
Map I for locations of capitals of states.)

The outer states found it expedient in dealing with
the inner states to adopt the modes and patterns for
intercourse which had become common practice for the
Chung-kuo.Thus we find that the Chin state was very
early admitted to the inner circle and became one of the
protectors of the ritual leadership of Chou. We have very
little information about the dealings of the outer states
with each other, for the main sources on this period such
as the Tso-chuan are concerned chiefly with the Chou
states. This is especially true for the periods I and II
when contacts reported by Tso were rather closely
limited to the central states.

MAP I

CAPITALS OF THE CH'UN-CH'IU STATES

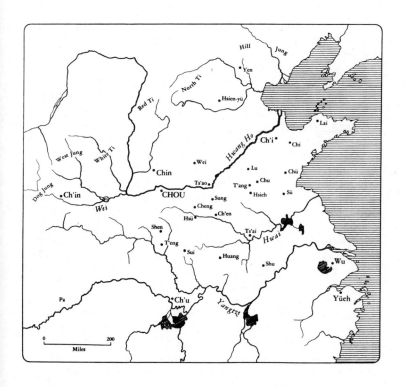

For sources see Chapter II, Note 32.

A number of Chinese students of international law,
who have been trained in the West, have analyzed the rudi-
ments of international law which existed in the Eastern
Chou period. We shall be more interested in some of
their findings when we discuss below some of the uniformities in the Ch'un-ch'iu system; we are mainly interested
here in pointing out that they agree almost unanimously
that there existed a system of sovereign states. The
latest of these studies, by Hung Chün-p'ei 洪鈞培, reviews
and summarizes most of the work by previous scholars
and musters a convincing array of proof in favor of the
sovereignty of the various states.[9] We need only call
attention to a few aspects.

It is necessary to point out again that the various
local groupings which constituted the main states of the
Ch'un-ch'iu were quite autonomous and independently
organized long before the start of that era. Professor
Wolfram Eberhard's studies have indicated that the Chou
period saw the development of a "Chinese" civilization
by virtue of the fact that at this time relations between
various local cultures were carried on with increasing
intensity.[10] It was understandable that these states should
insist upon maintaining their sovereignty. The whole of
the Lu chronicle argues that the various states were
sovereign units. Occasionally the power of a greater
state would make itself felt in the councils of the smaller
and would affect policy decisions there, but on the whole
the states guarded their sovereign powers jealously.
They waged war on each other, changed allies, and made
treaties to their own interest whenever possible. In 595
B.C. an incident is recorded by Tso which indicates the
extent to which even a small state valued its sovereignty.
It was customary for envoys to obtain permission for
passage through the states which lay in the path of their
missions. Envoys who attempted to pass without permission were seized and some were put to death. Knowing
this, the great state of Ch'u sent an envoy to Ch'i without
first obtaining permission for him to pass through Sung,
which lay on the route. Ch'u did this with the express
purpose of having an excuse to invade Sung if the envoy
were put to death. The Sung minister Hua Yüan 華元
knowing that Sung was being provoked said to his ruler:
"To pass through our State without asking our permission,
is to treat our State as if it were a border (dependency) of

Ch'u--is to deal with it as if Sung were not a State. If we put to death its messenger, Ch'u is sure to invade us, and Sung will perish. In either case Sung ceases to be a State."[11] Nevertheless, Sung put the messenger to death. The small state preferred to risk extinction at the hands of the powerful neighbor to the south rather than lose its sovereignty by infringement.

Another interesting example of the insistence upon sovereign rights by a small state occurred in Cheng in 523 B. C. One of the officers of the state died, and the powerful state of Chin to the north tried to have appointed a successor who would be favorably inclined toward itself. The Cheng statesman Tzu-ch'an 子産 warned his ruler, "If when any of the ministers of our ruler leaves the world, the great officers of Chin must determine who shall be his successor, this is to make Cheng a district or border (dependency) of Chin:--it ceases to be a State."[12]

In their relations with one another the states of the Ch'un-ch'iu were under no illusions about what did and did not constitute a state. Those states which maintained their sovereignty were treated as equals no matter what their size or nature. Treaties were made with the outer barbarian tribes on a footing of equality because those tribes managed to maintain their independence. Thus in 640 B. C. Ch'i made a treaty with the Ti 狄 for the purpose of relieving the state of Hsing 邢 which was under attack by Wei, and in 601 B. C. Chin made a covenant with the White Ti 白狄 to attack the state of Ch'in.[13] There was also no question but that before a territory could be considered a state, it had to have an effective political organization. The chronicle reports that in the winter of 684 B. C. "an army of Ch'i extinguished (mieh 滅) T'an 譚 and the Viscount of T'an fled to Chü 莒 ." To this the Kung Yang commentary adds in typical style, "Why does it not say left [T'an and went to Chü] ?--the country was already extinguished so there was no place to leave."[14] At the great conference which was held in 546 B. C. among most of the states, Chu 邾 had to all intents and purposes lost its independence in action to Ch'i as had T'eng 滕 to Sung, so it was decided that they should not sign the forthcoming treaty. The Lu representative observed, "Chu and T'eng are like the private possessions of other States. We are States among them. Why should we be put on the same footing as those?"[15]

According to the classes which were set up under the
original Chou feudal system, the states were ranked at
conferences and various diplomatic functions according
to the original patent or Chüeh 爵 conferred upon the
ruler by the Chou house. There were five ranks given:
Kung 公, Hou 侯, Po 伯, Tzu 子, and Nan 男, which are
generally translated in order, duke, marquis, earl, viscount,
and baron.[16] This ranking seems to hold for the first two
periods, but by the time we come to Period III in the
chronicle, it becomes obvious that the states are ranked
at conferences according to their power positions. Thus
at a conference of the states which was held at Yu 幽 in
678 B. C., the Ch'un-ch'iu reports the rulers ranked in
the following order: the Marquis of Ch'i, the Duke of Sung,
the Marquises of Ch'en and Wei, the Earl of Cheng, the
Baron of Hsü 許, the Earl of Hua 滑, and the Viscount of
T'eng.[17] By the time of the Ch'un-ch'iu patents of nobility had little practical meaning. Each of the rulers of the
Chou states was given the honorary title of Duke after his
death no matter what his original rank.

We are dealing then with a period of self-seeking
states, each with its own pride and ambition. The Lu
chronicle records the events in terms of the Chou system--
or what remained of it. It is, however, more profitable to
change the focus occasionally and to view these same
events from the point of view of the interests of the individual states with regard to specific incidents. One of the
first persons to study the Ch'un-ch'iu period from this
point of view was the Jesuit scholar Albert Tschepe. He
wrote histories of four of the great states of the epoch,
making them, so to speak, 'national' histories. His works,
besides offering very readable accounts of the period,
give further proof that in the Spring and Autumn era there
was a thorough-going sovereign state system in the north
and central part of the area now referred to by the general term China.[18]

Let us look a bit more closely at the process of consolidation which was taking place in Ancient China. It
becomes increasingly apparent that a great amount of this
consolidation was at the expense of what little control even
of a ceremonial nature the Chou ruler possessed. Already
in 707 B. C., there was a battle between Chou and Cheng
over the control of some land. By 652 we find the succes-

sion in Chou being determined by a group of the more powerful states.[19] On several occasions the Chou king was forced to reward his nominal vassals for saving him from complete extermination by giving them tracts of his ever-diminishing royal domain. Meanwhile the states went on expanding their areas and consolidating their power. The following table (Table II) lists the number of states absorbed by some of the greater powers according to the two scholars, Ku Tung-kao of the Ch'ing dynasty and a contemporary scholar, Li Tung-fan:[20]

TABLE II

State	Rank Under Chou System	States Conquered or Absorbed According to*	
		Ku Tung-kao	Li Tung-fang
Lu	Marquis	9	12
Sung	Duke	6	9
Wei	Marquis	3	7
Ch'i	Marquis	10	14
Chin	Earl	18	43
Ch'u	Viscount	42	32
Wu	Viscount	5	6
Yen	Earl	1	1

*The discrepancies in the two sets of figures are probably caused by different conclusions as to which of the conquered states actually continued as independent units after peace had been made. Ku evidently accepts the common view that the more totalitarian state of Ch'u absorbed completely the states which it conquered.

Although the table is by no means complete, the trend during the Ch'un-ch'iu shows up very plainly. The smaller states developed into buffer areas between those states which were enlarging the scope of their political control and were later to be absorbed by them. Thus, we even find Ts'ao, one of the states to consolidate its position early in the game, being absorbed in 487 B.C., by the Sung state. The greatest expansion of territory was that of Chin. It expanded its area beyond the point where control of an

effective nature could be maintained with any ease, and
soon after the end of the Ch'un-ch'iu (in 403 B.C.), it
broke up into three new states, Han 韓 , Wey 魏, and
Chao 趙 .

Confucius' own state of Lu was fairly successful in
consolidating its power and maintaining its area. Its
position as a power was hampered because of the fact
that it maintained many feudal vestiges, one of which was
a division of power within the state among three families
which were constantly striving for control. This was
compensated for in part by the prestige value of the close
connection with the former Chou power, and by the fact
that the internal divisions did not prevent some expansion
of territory. There are 18 entries in the chronicle concerning new land taken over by Lu. That Lu also maintained a fairly constant state of military preparedness
can be seen from the quite regular spacing in the Ch'un-
ch'iu of notices that Lu walled no less than twenty-six
towns.

The officers and statesmen of the time were completely aware of the process which was in motion and
knew that their states must follow the pattern if they
were to survive. In 579 B.C. a minister of Chin bemoaned
the struggle for territory in no uncertain terms: "The
princes are full of covetous greed, indulge their ambitious
desires without shrinking, and for a few feet of territory
will destroy their people, taking their martial officers and
using them to carry out their hearts' purposes as arms
and legs, as claws and teeth."[23] Yet thirty-five years
later in 544 B.C., a statesman of the same state pointed
out to his ruler that Chin's own greatness was attributable
to the fact that it had encroached upon the small states.[24]
In 548, the famous statesman and diplomat Tzu-ch'an
子產 of Cheng reported at the Chin court a victory over
Ch'en by his state. A Chin officer asked Tzu-ch'an why
Cheng had encroached upon a small state. His rejoinder
was to ask the Chin officer, "If you did not encroach upon
small States, how have you reached this extent of territory?"[25] The smaller states realized that their best
possible way to survive was to be on the winning side in
case of conflict. It was the duty of their statesmen to
determine which way the wind was blowing and get on the
right side regardless of prior treaties or agreements. An
officer of one of the small states observed, "Chin and Ch'u

make no effort to show kindness (to smaller States), but
keep struggling for superiority;--there is no reason why
we should not take the side of the first comer. They have
no faith;--why should we show good faith."[26]

Perhaps the best way to look at this process of state
expansion and the other changes which it brought with it
is to examine somewhat more intensively its course in
one state. The state of Ch'i forms an excellent example,
for it was the first state to achieve hegemony over the
Chou states and to organize a league to oppose the growing
power of Ch'u in the South. Map II indicates what a
faithful picture of the expansion of Ch'i is given by the
Ch'un-ch'iu and Tso-chuan. By locating the Ch'i towns as
mentioned year by year and drawing lines on the map
connecting the outer points in each of four Periods (I-III,
IV-VI, VII-IX, and X-XII) we get a very clear picture of
steady growth.

What were the methods by which this growth was
accomplished? In Ch'i's case it was almost entirely by
warfare.[27] In the case of acquisition by force, the incidents are usually listed in the chronicle as mieh 滅
"extinguished" or "destroyed", ch'ü 取 "seized",
chiang 降 "brought to terms", and ch'ien 遷 "removed".
Thus in 567 B.C. Ch'i extinguished Lai 萊 and T'ang
棠 ; in 549 B.C. it seized Chieh-ken 介根 ; in 664 B.C.
it brought Chang 鄣 to terms; and in 660 B.C. it removed
Yang 陽 . In one case a noble of the small principality of
Chi 紀 transferred his loyalty to Ch'i and handed over the
territory which he controlled, Hsi 郱 (692 B.C.). There
were, of course, other ways in which territory changed
hands. There was the indirect method of first establishing a protectorate over a territory and then annexing it
sometime later. In 655 B.C., Chin established a protectorate over the state of Yü 虞 when its armies passed
through it in order to attack Kuo 虢 . The victory over
Kuo made the absorption of Yü three years later a fore-
gone conclusion.[28] In 645 B.C. Chin paid a ransom of
eight cities for its ruler who had been seized by the
people of Ch'in.[29] There are also cases of exchange and
purchase of territory given in the Tso-chuan.

It was not Ch'i's territorial expansion, however,
which made it the first to gain a fairly effective control
over the central states. It was the process of political
centralization of power and rapid elimination of most of

MAP II

THE EXPANSION OF THE STATE OF CH'I DURING

THE CH'UN-CH'IU PERIOD

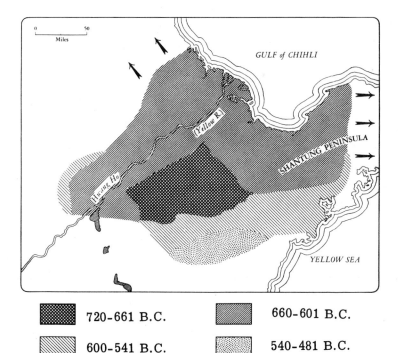

720-661 B.C.   660-601 B.C.

600-541 B.C.   540-481 B.C.

The area for each period is determined by connecting the outermost locations mentioned in the text of the Ch'un ch'iu and the Tso-chuan. Thus, the map does not necessarily indicate all the area controlled by Ch'i. It is quite probable that by the end of the Ch'un-ch'iu period it had expanded far to the east and north in the areas indicated by the small arrows (→) on the map. For Ch'i's location with respect to the other states, see Map I.

the vestiges of internal feudalism which made Ch'i the
dominant power from 681-643 B.C. The centralization of
state power was the logical continuation of a pattern
which had been developing since the earliest days of the
civilization which existed in the Yellow River valley.[30]
The decline in any real political meaning of the feudal
ties with Chou, the general process of state expansion, the
fact that Ch'i had fewer autonomous vassals than the other
states, and Ch'i's situation on a plain where the communication necessary for control was fairly easy: all these
aided in the early reaction of a centralized regime.[31]
But the main credit for the emergence of Ch'i as a great
power goes to Duke Huan 桓公 and his able advisor Kuan
Chung 管仲 (Kuan Yi-wu 管夷吾) who is perhaps best
known as the Philosopher Kuan or Kuan-tzu 管子 .

Kuan-tzu has been hailed as China's first economist,
as the first state-maker in Chinese history, as the first
great philosopher, etc. , and there is a lengthy book which
has come down to us bearing his name in which he has
lengthy discussions with his ruler over proposed measures
for reform in Ch'i. Since he was obviously not a Confu-
cianist, this work was probably not changed much to fit in
with Confucian tradition by the Han systematizers; but
most of it is probably spurious, and it can hardly be considered a reliable source for a consideration of the work
of Kuan Chung.[32] There are, however, sufficient data to
be gleaned from free texts to provide a general outline of
the accomplishments of this statesman and show how they
affected the course of events in Ancient China.[33]

The reforms in the government of the state of Ch'i
carried out by Duke Huan under the guidance of his able
minister may be conveniently classed under three general
headings: administrative, military, and economic.
Throughout his ministry Kuan-tzu had the complete con-
fidence of his ruler, so he was able to carry out most of
his rather strict measures with the utmost vigor. In fact,
he has been fairly generally condemned by the Confucian-
ists for his somewhat legalistic methods. Ssu-ma Ch'ien
remarks in his biography of Kuan-tzu, "As to the character
of Kuan-Chung, the world called him a wise minister, but,
Confucius said he was a small man. Is it because he
assisted Duke Huan, that good prince, to establish supremacy by force and not by moral power?"[35]

The system of ministers and officials which prevailed

during the early Ch'un-ch'iu period among most of the
states of the central area is perhaps best exemplified by
the organization in the State of Sung which is discussed
in several places in the Tso-chuan. The government of
the state was carried on by six main officials all of whom
were rather autonomous members of noble families within
the state. Although the ruler was the head of the state his
control over these officials was relatively weak, so that
together with the ruler these officials constituted a board
of seven officers whose powers are not clearly defined.
In addition to the supposedly specialized duties which
these officers performed, each as a vassal was in charge
of a section of the country. This meant that there could
hardly be an efficient centralized administration on any
issue where the local interests of one or more of these
officials might conflict. These officers were: the com-
manders of the two armies of the state of Sung, Left
Tso 左 and Right Yu 右 ; the Minister of War Ssu-ma
司馬 ; the Minister of Instruction Ssu-t'u 司徒 ; the
Minister of Works Ssu-ch'eng 司城 ; and the Minister of
Crime Ssu-k'ou 司寇 (called Ssu-k'ung 司空 in the other
Chou states).36 The military system and organization in
these states was also on a rather haphazard basis, so
that in battle they could hardly ever present a completely
united front.

The weaknesses apparent in these two aspects, the
political and military, were the first items listed for
change by Kuan-tzu. His first measure was to divide the
population of the state into 21 divisions, or hsiang 鄉, for
administrative purposes. Six of these hsiang were
functional and were made up of the craftsmen, literati,
and merchants who were given special privileges. The
other 15 were regional and were made up of the peasants
throughout the land. These were organized into three
groups of five each. Each of these hsiang was carefully
divided and subdivided so as to establish a direct line of
responsibility right to the top. The leaders of the hsiang
or Hsiang-chang 鄉長 were required to report once a
year to the Ch'i ruler on the conditions in their area of
control. They were encouraged to appoint the leaders of
the various subdivisions on merit rather than privilege.37
Kuan-tzu also set up a system of inspectors to check on
the work of the officials of various grades--perhaps the
forerunner of the famous Chinese censoral system.38

Within this administrative organization Duke Huan, under the guidance of Kuan-tzu, established a militia system. Each family was required to furnish one soldier, and these soldiers were grouped in the same divisions and subdivisions as the government of the state. The three political divisions of five hsiang each thus contributed three great armies. This enabled the people to have a certain pride in the militia of their division and also in turn a pride in their state. The result of all this was a happy combination of divided authority under a centralized administration, and, of course, a new power for Ch'i.[39] The new centralized power of the prince was perhaps best exemplified by the position of Kuan-tzu himself. His office was that of Hsiang 相 . Before Kuan-tzu initiated his changes the function of the Hsiang had been to make sure that the ruler carried out the ritual ceremonies in proper order. He was the private officer of the ruler. The post had not been one of very great importance, but as other states followed the Ch'i pattern, the office came more and more to be that of a Prime Minister. As one modern scholar has observed, "use of his private official to control the administration of the country was a manifestation of the growing central power of the ruler."[40]

On the economic side Kuan-tzu's changes were perhaps even more revolutionary. He laid a foundation which enabled Ch'i to maintain its position as a strong power long after the initial vigor of the political and military changes had worn off. The Shih-chi reports that Kuan-tzu controlled prices, corrected the system of weights and measures, encouraged commerce, accumulated wealth and enriched the country.[41] One of the measures which enabled the central government to accumulate wealth was a salt monopoly which was instituted at this time. Kuan-tzu also established a government monopoly on iron. The iron monopoly enabled Duke Huan to maintain an effective control of arms within the state, and the salt monopoly strengthened his power over the masses. Not only were Ch'i merchants encouraged to carry on trade outside the country, but, together with the artisans, they were exempted from military service so that they might continue their work which Kuan-tzu deemed vital for the power of the country.[42]

Just at this time the State of Ch'u to the south began to exhibit ambitious designs on the territory of the Chou

states. The Ch'i ruler, because of the internal strength
of his own state was able to assemble the princes of the
others to oppose Ch'u's armies which were invading
Cheng. By 679 B. C. a representative of the Chou king
added ritual importance to the conclave of the rulers by
his presence and Duke Huan was officially recognized as
pa 霸 or protector.[43] He had purposely cultivated the
friendship of his neighbors by returning at first some of
the lands which had been seized from them by former
Ch'i rulers. He then marked out the boundaries of his
state very carefully so that the other rulers would have
no apprehensions about his designs on them and would
know that their sovereign rights were secure. The result
was that there was very little dispute about his right to
assume the leadership of the Chou states.[44] At the meeting at Shao-ling 召陵 in 656 B. C. Duke Huan was able to
assemble the princes of eight other states. The Ch'un-
ch'iu and Tso-chuan record 24 meetings hui 會 attended
by Duke Huan during the period of his leadership, 681-
644 B. C.[45]

These great changes in the State of Ch'i constitute
one of the most important developments in the history of
Chinese government.[46] The pattern established by Ch'i
spread to the other larger states which had been somewhat blindly seeking a method which would enable them
effectively to govern their growing areas. The new
organization which was established by the famous protector Duke Wen 文 of Chin (635-628 B. C.)was essentially that of Kuan Chung and Duke Huan.[47] The Tso-chuan
reports on the reorganization of administration in several
of the states: among others Ch'u[48], Chin[49], Cheng[50], and
even Lu itself.[51]

Still another aspect of this process was the replace-
ment of older internal rules and forms--the li 禮 --by a
systematic code of laws--fa 法 . This change from li to
fa has been pointed out by several of the modern Chinese
scholars. It was necessitated by the growth in complexity
of social organization, the changing class structure, and
the increasing wealth which needed new forms of protection.[52] In 543 B. C., there is an account of a new system
of laws which was instituted by Tzu-ch'an in Cheng; and
in 512 B. C. , there is a record of the inscription of the
new laws of Chin on some bronze vessels.[53]

All this helped to eliminate divided control and to

centralize state power in the person or symbol of the
ruler. The trend can easily be followed through the pages
of the Lu chronicles. In some states there was less
trouble with independent vassals within the area controlled by the prince. That drawback was suffered mainly
by the former Chou states. There is not, for example, a
single mention of internal strife within the state of Ch'in
to the west. The ruling house there maintained a strong
control from early days. But even in the Chou states
most of the vestiges of divided feudal authority had been
virtually eliminated by the end of the Spring and Autumn
times. In some cases the ruler himself was the active
leader of more unified control; in others the newly arising
class of government officials used the symbolic attraction
of the prince to organize the state on a basis of centralized
administration.[54]

The importance of this shift to larger areas of political control and to increasing rigor in its exercise cannot
be stressed too much. It was necessary to have this
administrative experience and to develop these new political patterns before it could ever be possible to govern the
whole of what was to become China. Indeed, it can safely
be maintained that without this background of development
in the Ch'un-ch'iu period the unification of China under
Ch'in Shih Huang in 221 B. C. could never have taken
place. Perhaps Kuan-tzu did more to aid the Ch'in cause
than did Lord Shang or Li Ssu. This is the proposition
advanced by Tung Shu-yeh in one of the most scholarly
modern studies of the history of this period. He says,
"Day by day the original feudal organization was destroyed
and the pattern for the scope of unification under the Ch'in
and Han was laid in this time."[55]

Along with this process of state expansion and centralization came the development of patterns of increasing
loyalty to the state, or patriotism. This new patriotism
came as a logical result of, and in turn aided and abetted,
original localism. Broad differences in dialect, customs,
religion, legends, and cults, have been shown to have
existed among the various regions prior to the Ch'un-
ch'iu.[56] In the Ch'un-ch'iu we find a growing awareness
of those differences as contacts increased, and also the
development of a certain pride in local origins and dis-
tinctions. Careful reading of the Tso commentary indicates a gradual transference of the symbol of the loyalty

of the peasant from the feudal lord directly over him to
the person of the prince of the state and the state itself.
The very fact that the states were sovereign and insisted
on maintaining that sovereignty contributed to the local
pride. It has already been pointed out that each of the
states had its own annals and records. Improvements in
transportation aided in creating unity within the states
themselves, but the transport system was still not to the
stage where it could aid in eliminating the wide cultural
differences between states and the patterns of patriotism
which had become firmly established by the end of the
Ch'un-ch'iu period.[57]

Of course, a great amount of this patriotism grew
out of the struggles which went on among the states in
their efforts to maintain their existence; from their
battles fought in the name of preservation; and their
efforts to curb the expansion of other states. Jealousies
naturally were engendered, and these in turn stimulated
feelings of unity and enforced the patriotism. As early
as 683 B. C. for example, we find the Duke of Sung
speaking to one of his subjects released from capture by
Lu. The two states had been at war over a period of
years. He said, "Formerly, I respected you; but since you
have been a prisoner of Lu, I respect you no more."[58]
The greatest cultural differences existed between the
state of Ch'u in the south and the northern states. The
Ch'u people were proud of their distinctive music, ceremonies, and traditions. We have seen that the architecture
was so attractive that the Duke of Lu, after a visit to Ch'u,
built himself a palace patterned after those he had seen.
The classical commentators have nothing but condemna-
tion for this, and it seems to them a just retribution that
he should die in his new "foreign style" palace. [59]

In 582 B. C., the state of Chin captured a Ch'u
musician. The Chin ruler was so impressed not only with
the beauty of the distinctive southern tunes, but also with
the patriotism of this man, who would yield no information to his captor, that he released him.[60]

The expression by individuals of their loyalty to
particular states illustrates better than argument the
advanced disintegration of the feudal power of Chou,
which was no longer much more than nominal. Indeed, the
symbolic ritual attraction became weaker and weaker.
In 632 B. C., one officer of Ch'u observed to another,

"If by dying you could benefit the State, peradventure you
would do it."[61] Again in 496 B. C. , a lord of one of the
three families which were struggling for supremacy in
the state of Chin stated, "If by my death the State of Chin
get repose and the Chao family be established, why should
I live?"[62] The expression of loyalty to the state came
first. The culmination of this trend toward increasing
patriotism was reached after the close of the Ch'un-
ch'iu period when the rulers of the various states pro-
claimed themselves kings (wang 王) and the real battle
for complete control of the Chinese cultural area reached
its final stage. During this later Chan-kuo period the
expressions of loyalty to and interest in the state abound.
A great number of the conversations recorded by Mencius
are with a ruler who is seeking ways of increasing the
loyalty of his subjects as a means of increasing the power
of his state, Ch'i.[63] It is perhaps not without significance
that today a scholar from Shantung will refer to himself
as a man of Ch'i. This growth of patriotic devotion to the
state no doubt explains why, after he had conquered these
states one by one, the first emperor of a unified China
found it necessary to burn all their books and local
records (213 B. C.).

The development of patriotism made it increasingly
difficult for the larger powers to absorb even the smallest
neighbors. Thus, throughout the Ch'un-ch'iu period we
find different methods of control developing. Ultimately
a state's position was determined by its place in this control fabric, which makes it desirable to outline here in
brief some of these methods. There were first of all the
great powers which owed allegiance to no one. Through
most of the Ch'un-ch'iu period these were: Ch'i, Chin,
Ch'in, Ch'u, and Wu. Occasionally Ch'i, Chin, and Ch'in
expressed a formal submission to Chou, but this was
usually only because it was politically desirable to do
so.[64] Ch'i had initiated a pattern during its tenure of
hegemony, continued during that of Chin, which lasted
through most of the remainder of the Ch'un-ch'iu period.
This pattern was to proclaim the support of Chou institutions so as to allay the misgivings of the smaller states
about the ambitions of the hegemon. These smaller states,
it was hoped, would then join with it in opposing its
stronger rivals outside the Chou area. One writer has
characterized the policies followed by the league of states

formed under the royal blessing of Chou as status quo policies.[65] After Ch'i had lost to Chin the leadership of the central states, it realized that its position would be strengthened by remaining outside the league, and it tried to do this whenever possible. The strong financial position which Kuan-tzu had helped to create frequently enabled it to buy its independence from the league by bribes, as, for example, it did in 612 B. C.[66] In addition to being able to convoke meetings of the central states and direct most of their policies and actions outside the Chou area, the leader of the Chou League, who was known as meng-chu 盟主 or "President of the Covenants," received tribute from the states which he led.[67]

Below the great powers were the states of secondary magnitude. These insisted on certain sovereign rights and, especially in the Chou area, tolerated little interference by the great powers in their relations with each other. These were the states like Lu, Ts'ao, Sung, and Wei. They stood a far greater chance of maintaining their autonomy under the Chou system than did those in the league controlled by Ch'u in the south throughout most of the period. The secondary powers on the edges of Ch'u's area of influence attempted to switch their political alignment away from Ch'u whenever possible. For example, in 648 B. C. the states of Huang 黃 and Chiang 江 signed a treaty with Duke Huan of Ch'i, who was only too happy to have them come over to his side. Ch'u subsequently invaded and extinguished them; they waited in vain for aid from Ch'i which was too far to the north.[68]

Below the great and secondary powers were the attached states fu-yung 附庸 and colonies shu 屬 . The attached states were smaller and owed existence and allegiance directly to one of the larger powers. According to Mencius these states were less than fifty square li 里 (about eight square English miles) in area and did not have direct access to the Chou court.[69] This is probably too formal a classification, but in any case these were usually not accorded equal treatment. Below them were the destroyed states which had been made into provinces of the larger units. Sometimes they managed to maintain their names or later to re-emerge as independent political entities, but such was not often the case. Ch'u was the power most notorious for eliminating the states which it conquered and making hsiang 鄉 or provinces of them, as for example, in 534 B. C., when it conquered Ch'en 陳 and made it a part of its own territory.[70] Other great powers in addition to Ch'u also kept newly conquered territories intact as administrative areas. Such practices were followed by Ch'in, Chin, Ch'i, and Wu. Here, indeed, may have been the origin of the Hsien-chün system of administrative subdivisions instituted by the Ch'in rulers several centuries later.[71]

It is difficult to decide just what the reasons were for this process of state expansion and consolidation, a process which went on all through the Ch'un-ch'iu period and continued with increasing intensity until 221 B. C. In search of an explanation, some of the Chinese philosophers turned to an examination of man's basic nature.[72] Surely the insecurities engendered by the constant rivalry between Ch'u and the Chou states accounted for some of the aggression, as, for example, in the case of Huang and Chiang cited above. The ambitions of leaders, of course, played a part. Pride, buttressed by the growing patriotism, accounted for battles in which the weaker were overcome by the stronger as in the case of Lu's extinction of K'uei 夔 in 634 B. C. One thing is certain: there was little doubt in the minds of any of the statesmen of the time that a state must be strong if it were to survive. The Tso-chuan records the following conversation of 583 B. C.:

> The marquis of Chin sent Wu-ch'en, duke of Shen, on a mission to Wu. Having asked leave to pass through Chü, he was standing with duke Ch'ü-ch'iu above the city-moat, and said to him, '"The wall is in a bad condition.' The viscount of Chü replied, 'Chü is a poor State, lying among the wild tribes of the east; who would think of taking any measures against me?' Wu-ch'en said, 'Crafty men there are who think of enlarging boundaries for the advantage of the altars of their States;--what State is there which has not such men? It is thus that there are so many large States. Some think (there may be dangers); some let things take their course. But a brave man keeps the leaves of his door shut;--how much more should a State do so!'[73]

It is perhaps best then to turn to an examination of

the elements which helped to constitute a strong and
secure state. In expanding their territory and bidding for
the control of the smaller states, the great powers had to
calculate on the amount and strength of the opposition.
In general, large campaigns were not carried out without
first making an assessment of the situation. Thus it is
desirable to know what constituted the main components
of power of a given state or alliance of states at any
particular time. It is also important to examine the extent to which these components of state power were
appreciated by the statesmen of the time. The latter
could have just as important a part in determining the
course of events as the former.

Chapter IV

THE COMPONENTS OF POWER

As might be expected, the determination of the
relative power of the various Ch'un-ch'iu states was no
simple matter; a multiplicity of factors was involved.
Yet, in a time when the weaker states were rapidly being
extinguished by the stronger, the measurement of power
was important to all states which hoped to preserve their
own existence. The final measurement, of course, was the
actual power test--war. Here the raw power potential
was likely to weigh most heavily. This was made up of
what are sometimes termed the "elements of power."
Which of these weighed most heavily was in turn determined by the methods of warfare. We shall term this raw
power potential of the states the "tangible component of
power" in order to distinguish it from other factors in
their power makeup which we shall describe below under
the respective terms "intangible component" and "contextual
component."

The most easily measured item in the tangible component of state power in the Ch'un-ch'iu was the standing
military establishment. Here the commonly accepted
method of ranking the Ch'un-ch'iu states was by the
number of four-horse chariots which they could muster.
Even today the translation of the term "great power" is
commonly rendered wan-ch'eng-kuo 萬乘國 "a country of
ten thousand four-horse chariots." In order to understand
why this should be the common denominator for measuring
the military establishments of the various states, it is
perhaps best to give a brief sketch of war as it was
carried on in Ancient China.

Each army built its power in the field around a large
chariot drawn by four mailed horses. The chariot itself
was not so much the instrument of battle; it was a convey-
ance for the leader. Surrounding each chariot were from
thirty to seventy-five men. In the chariot were three men:
the leader, who stood on the left, the driver in the middle,
and the spearman on the right. Also in the chariot were

a drum, a bell or gong, and a flag on a long pole. These
three items were used to direct the men from the vantage
point above them in the chariot. The drum was used to
signal a general advance and the movements to the right
and left in the advance. In the heat of a battle when the
drums of hundreds of chariots were sounding--it must
have been almost as deafening as a modern artillery
barrage--the flag was used for signalling troop movements. The bell was reserved for signalling retreats.
The spearman in the chariot was normally able to protect
the leader--usually of noble birth--and there were seldom
many casualties among the men in the chariot.[1] Some of
the chariots were used as weapons to aid the men on the
ground. They carried large knives attached to the axle-
heads which with proper maneuvering could be used with
great effectivemess against the enemy militia.[2]

Most of the casualties were suffered by the men on
the ground around the chariots. Foot troops of the larger
and more prosperous states wore some armor, but the
majority had to depend for survival on their skill with the
weapons which they had at their disposal. Weapons used
included the ko 戈 spear, mao 矛 halberd, chien 劍 sword,
chi 戟 lance, tao 刀 knife, fu 斧 axe, yüeh 鉞 battle-axe,
and kung-chien 弓箭 bow and arrow. The items of defen-
sive armor such as shields, helmets, etc. were largely
ineffective.[3] The development of the use of iron for
weapons was one of the important changes which affected
the status of some of the states. Ch'i and Chin with their
superior resources had the edge on that score. Until the
end of the period, however, bronze weapons continued in
active use.[4] These battles based upon the use of the
chariot and the men around it were no small affairs. The
state of Chin, for example, is reported at one time to have
had 4,900 chariots employed in the field.[5]

Important to the military power of the states were
their walled cities with their moats. Sieges of some of
these cities lasted for months. They formed admirable
places for retreat, and usually the attacking army had to
retire from the siege because of lack of supplies. The
walling of towns and cities usually indicated a feeling of
insecurity on the border near which the town was situated.
For example, in 707 B. C. , Lu walled a town near the Ch'i
border in anticipation of an attack from Ch'i.[6] Likewise,
it was frequently advisable to wall a town on the border as

a place of retreat from an unsuccessful attack upon an
enemy country. Quite often the enemy decided to follow
up its advantage. It was for this reason that Lu walled
the town of Ch'i 漆 before attacking Chu in 495 B. C.[7]
Thus the number of walled cities constituted an important part of a state's military establishment. The walling
of a city took great expenditures of effort and time and
was accordingly treated as an important event. Of course,
most important of all was the capital city of a state. It
was the symbol of state power, and chances were that its
fall would mean the utter defeat of the state. Few states
had cities equally well fortified or equal in size to their
capitals. [8]

In some of the southern states the navy formed an
important part of the military establishment. Toward the
close of the Ch'un-ch'iu a great number of the military
encounters between the states of Wu and Ch'u were naval
engagements like, for example, the battles of 523 and 518
B. C.[9] In the south the many rivers and lakes formed the
most effective avenues of transportation. In the north the
soldiers used the roads, but often supplies were shipped
by canal. The troops occasionally used the canals too.[10]
The Yellow River could be used to some extent for transport; in 647 B. C., Tso reports a shipment of grain from
Ch'in to Chin by boat.[11]

In addition to the standing military establishment
there were other times in the tangible component of state
power which were relatively easy to calculate. Obviously
the population was among these. On this score, however,
there is practically no reliable information available
today. The Chinese have never been deeply concerned
about making accurate tabulations of population. Very few
studies of the population of the Ch'un-ch'iu period have
been made, and those which exist usually accent the population for all of China--sticking to the ideal of Chou
unity--rather than that of the various states.[12] About the
only person to give figures for the period has been the
Russian scholar, T. Sacharoff, but he gives no indication
of how these figures were obtained. He estimates that in
685 B. C., the population of China was about twelve
million.[13] We do know that the population of the various
states determined in large measure the number of men
they could put onto the field of battle, and that the statesmen of the Spring and Autumn times had little difficulty

in picking out which were the Great Powers on the latter
score. Toward the close of the period the states of Chin
and Ch'u were each putting over 100,000 men in the
field.[14]

Likewise the geographical area and position of the
various states was an item the importance of which could
readily be appreciated. Stress has already been placed
upon the fact that certain of the outer states had comparatively large buffer areas into which they could expand
their power and extend their control without great opposition. This fact has been noticed by many writers.[15]
Toward the end of the Ch'un-ch'iu, after the main process
of expansion and consolidation had taken place, the areas
controlled by such powerful states as Ch'i, Chin, and
Ch'u were almost equal to pre-World War II France or
Germany.[16] Certain territories were more easily defended
than others, and there was a very realistic appreciation
of the value of obtaining various strategic points. In 658
B.C., Chin occupied the city of Hsia-yang 夏陽, which
made the reduction of Kuo 虢 and Yü 虞 practically inevitable. Hsia-yang, an excellent fortress in an ideal
geographical situation, was the exception to the observation
made on capital cities above.[17] In 596 B.C., the Chin
ruler announced to his ministers how secure he felt his
state to be. One of the first items which he cataloged was
Chin's possession of many high mountains and narrow
passes in the loessal highlands.[18]

Largely dependent upon the geography and also of
vital importance was the economic productivity of the
various states in which agriculture played the main role.
In the early years of the Ch'un-ch'iu, grain raids constituted one of the chief types of periodic incursions made
by one state into the territory of another.[19] The states
soon developed central storehouses, however, and there
are many records of one state selling grain to another
which was hard-pressed.[20] With the many improvements
in tillage of the soil during the Ch'un-ch'iu the larger
states were able to divert their activities to luxury construction and more concentration on state armaments as
grain surpluses began to accumulate. Crops were especially abundant in Ch'u.[21] Animal husbandry played an
important part since the method of warfare put a premium
on horses. In the incident already mentioned, the Chin
ruler listed the great number of horses in his state as the

second of his reasons for feeling secure. In 539 B. C. ,
it was said of the state of Yen, "She was never a strong
power despite her numerous horses!"[22]

By the closing years of the Ch'un-ch'iu, the Ch'i
statesman Yen-tzu 晏子 , a contemporary of Confucius,
observed in his pithy style that the large states cared
only for prestige while the smaller ones still had to concern themselves with production for day-to-day life.[23]
Industrial production--mainly of agricultural implements
and also of the weapons of war--assumed growing importance. The industrial foundations which were laid by Kuan-
tzu in Ch'i enabled that state to maintain a strong position
through most of the years of the Ch'un-ch'iu. At one point
the state of Ch'u hesitated to declare war on Chin because
of the rapid strides which the latter had made in industry.[24]

Commercial development was also an item of tangible
significance, though sometimes less easily measured. The
states of Ch'i and Cheng had the greatest number of
traders, as has already been pointed out; and they were
frequently able to buy themselves out of difficult situa-
tions.

The ability to bring to their fullest and most harmon-
ious development the factors which constituted the tangible
component of state power in Ancient China depended in
turn on what might be termed the "intangible component."
Several of the items which made up this intangible component may be conveniently listed under the heading of
'abilities'.

Naturally important was the ability to provide skill-
ful leadership, which involved the ability to create unity
and to gain the whole-hearted support of the people, as
well as to keep the friendship of allies. The Tso-chuan
abounds with stories of victory resulting from able
leadership, and defeat caused by its lack. Ch'i under
Kuan-tzu and Duke Huan is an excellent example of the
positive importance of constructive leadership. Soon after
these men died, it lost its place as the foremost state in
the Chou area. Ch'u provides examples of some weakness
in this field. The ruthlessness with which Ch'u treated
the smaller states in its orbit made them doubtful allies
when the course of battle seemed to go against Ch'u. In
519 B. C. , during a battle between Ch'u and Wu, the com-
mander of Ch'u's forces was killed. A Wu leader was
quick to see how fortunate this was for his cause:

The States that follow Ch'u are numerous, but
they are small. They have come through fear of
Ch'u, and because they could not help it.... the
courage of its army has become chilled.... The
seven states are engaged in the same service
but they have not the same heart.... Ch'u can be
defeated.[25]

Another example of recognition of the importance of
unity among the people is furnished by a Marquis of Wei.
In 502 B.C., he had one of his officers arrange for an
audience with the people. When they were assembled, he
asked them whether they would support him in revolting
from the leadership of the state of Chin: "If Wei revolts
from Chin, and Chin five times attacks us, how would you
bear the distress?" They replied, "Though it should five
times attack us, we should still be able to fight." Having
thus assured himself of the unity and support of his
people, the Wei ruler felt safe in breaking ties with the
much larger and stronger state, but which was at that
time having internal troubles.[26]

In 575 B.C., a statesman of Chin itself made a very
shrewd statement on the necessity for internal unity, and
one of the ways by which to secure it. At that time Chin
was near the peak of its power, and there was a possibility that with a long hard struggle it could bring to terms
Ch'u, the only remaining center of great opposition. But
Chin's newly-found allies were of questionable loyalty,
and one of the Chin statesmen realized the need for an
external threat to create unity in the league of states
headed by Chin. He observed to his ruler, "(In their
times), Ch'in, Ti, Ch'i, and Ch'u were all powerful enemies;
and if they had not exerted their strength, their descendants would have been reduced to weakness. But now three
of these strong ones have submitted, and we have only to
cope with Ch'u. It is only a sage ruler who can safely be
without trouble either from abroad or within his state.
Excepting under a sage ruler, when there is quietness
abroad, sorrow is sure to spring up at home; why not
leave Ch'u to be an occasion of apprehension to us from
abroad?"[27]

The reverse of this technique was used by the ruler
of Wei who thought of getting himself in favor with the
various strong rulers outside his country in order to

increase his support at home.[28] We have already noted
that part of the necessary internal unity came as a result of the growing centralization of state power under
more efficient administration, and with the growing
patriotism of Ch'un-ch'iu times.

Ability in diplomacy was also important for the
effective exercise of state power. Twice the little state
of Lu was able to get approval from Chin for its plans to
absorb smaller states. This was mainly because Lu diplomats at the Chin court were able to convince the Chin
ruler that it was to his own self interest to sanction it.[29]
In 630 B. C., an envoy from Cheng was able to persuade
the Ch'in ruler to withdraw his support from Chin's attack
on Cheng. He pointed out that a victory over Cheng was
really not in Ch'in's interest. Chin then gave up the
campaign, and hostilities ceased.[30] Again, in 634 B. C.,
Lu's ability in diplomacy was mainly responsible for preventing an attack by the superior power Ch'i.[31]

Necessary for success in both leadership and diplomacy was the ability to make a proper assessment of the
interstate situation. This required knowledge of internal
conditions in other states, in order to determine the
gravity of threats to the security of the home state. In
627 B. C., a Chin minister accurately pointed out to his
ruler that the threat to Chin's security lay in the west,
with the state of Ch'in, and not to the south.[32] There are
many instances in the Tso-chuan of attempts to get information from prisoners of war about conditions in their
countries. The Yen-tzu Ch'un-ch'iu gives a very interesting account of an incursion into the state of Lu by the
Ch'i ruler, to feel out Lu's defenses and to get information.
The Ch'i ruler questioned a prisoner, and from him
found out that the crops were expected to be especially
good in Lu that year. Since this meant that the people
would probably be well fed, and therefore united behind
their government, he decided not to attack Lu.[33] Tso also
gives several cases in which spies were sent out to gather
information from rival countries. For example, in anticipation of making an attack on Ch'u in 537 B. C., Wu sent
a spy there to find out what preparations by Wu would be
most effective.[34]

Another item in the intangible component of state
power was the prestige factor. We have pointed out how
Lu's close relationship to Chou gave it a certain claim to

special treatment --and especially among the central
states. This was the main reason why in 661 B. C. , Duke
Huan of Ch'i refrained from annexing the state.[36] The
rulers and statesmen of the Ch'un-ch'iu were well aware
of the importance to a state of its prestige. In 648 B. C.
Kuan-tzu advised Duke Huan against accepting the support
of the states of Chiang and Huang. He pointed out to his
ruler: "Chiang and Huang are far from Ch'i and near to
Ch'u, --states which Ch'u considers advantageous to it.
Should Ch'u attack them, and you not be able to save them,
you will cease to be looked up to by the States."[37] Similarly Chin withdrew from Cheng in 563 B. C. , without
meeting the Cheng army because it was pointed out by one
of its advisors that "If we now attack its (Cheng's) army,
Ch'u will come to its help. If we fight and do not conquer,
the States will laugh at us. Victory cannot be commanded.
We had better withdraw."[38]

The amount of prestige which a state was able to
build up largely determined to what extent it could count
on its allies, and this was another important part of the
intangible component of state power. Occasionally one of
the great powers could make an agreement with a smaller
state for a fixed amount of military aid, in which case the
factor was not quite such an intangible one. This was the
case in 500 B. C. , when Ch'i and Lu signed a treaty in
which Lu, in return for some territorial concessions
promised to furnish a force of 300 chariots for Ch'i for
any expedition which that state might conduct outside its
borders.   Usually, however, the support of allies was
an unknown quantity; and the great powers employed
every possible method to make sure that their satellites
would remain attached to them. As Tzu-ch'an observed,
"If a state does not show itself strong, it will be insulted
and no longer fit to be a state."[39] A standard practice
was to conduct large military reviews before the eyes of
visiting dignitaries in order to convince them of the great
power of their ally. In 671 B. C. , Ch'i put on such a military demonstration for the visiting ruler of Lu.[40] The
largest such demonstration of power for prestige purposes
and for securing allies was one staged by Chin in 529
B. C. , involving over 4000 chariots.[41]

Of course, the significance of the power, tangible or
intangible, which a state could muster, depended in large
measure upon its location with respect to the main centers

of power, the extent to which it was itself a center of
power, and the amount of opposition which it was likely to
encounter. This relativistic aspect of the power of the
various states of the Ch'un-ch'iu we shall call the "contextual component" of state power. It is perhaps advisable
to examine it in some detail before considering some
further examples of how Ch'un-ch'iu leaders assessed
their power position.

To this contextual component of state power the
leaders of the small states had to give closest attention
if they wished to maintain their sovereignty. The state of
Yen, located far to the north, could feel fairly secure
because of the great amount of buffer area between it and
the other great centers of power to the south. Yet toward
the close of period XI it was threatened by Ch'i's improvements in the modes of troop transport. The small states
situated between two large centers of power had to be sure
that they were on the winning side in any contest or their
continued existence was threatened. It was for this reason
that they were never certain allies for the great powers.
The smaller states well within the orbits of the great
powers had the difficult task of trying to maintain their
independence while still following the policies of the leading state. Such a state was Lu. The Ch'un-ch'iu and the
Tso-chuan are a record of its attempt to follow its own
policies and yet reconcile them with those of the great
powers among the Chou states, first Ch'i (from 681 to 643
B. C.) and then Chin (from 640 B. C. until about 510 B. C.).

The great powers themselves evaluated the contextual
component of their power by their ability to prevent any
one state trom getting enough power to upset the balance.
When, as in Ch'un-ch'iu times, each of the main power
centers was seeking to attain a position of superiority in
the tangible and intangible components of power, this
meant a concerted effort to prevent another state from
arriving at that position first. After Ch'i and Ch'u had
begun to emerge as the powerful leaders of the states,
such a balancing process went on through most of the
Spring and Autumn Period between the Chou states in the
Yellow River valley and the southern states in the Yangtze
River valley. The most intense rivalry, however, came
after 642 B. C. when Chin had replaced Ch'i as the leader
of the Chou states.

Throughout most of the Ch'un-ch'iu this balancing

process centered on the state of Cheng which occupied a
fairly extensive amount of territory from east to west
just between the two poles. In their attempt to attain a
position of superiority which would insure their security,
the leagues of states in the north and south usually fixed
upon the control of this state as the decisive factor.[42]
Cheng was not a weak state.[43] It is, in fact, the first state
mentioned in the Lu annals as annexing another state. It
took over the state of Hsi 息 in 712 B. C. In the first of
the twelve periods of the Ch'un-ch'iu Cheng was the power
which caused most apprehension among the Chou states.
We have noted above that its central position enabled it
to gain a commercial lead early in the period, and it
remained one of the leading commercial powers throughout. Cheng was also fortunate in having a long line of able
statesmen and also in being able to follow out policies of
centralization quite early. Its people developed a patriotism for the cause of their state which made its extinction
by any one of its more powerful neighbors practically
impossible. The most the neighboring states could hope
for was to control the external policies and alignment of
Cheng.

The Tso-chuan reports more extensively on the
intense rivalry between the two leagues of states centering
on Cheng, than any other series of events in Ancient China.
During periods III-IV the rivalry was between the Chou
states lead by Ch'i and the states loyal to Ch'u, and from
period V to period XI it was between Chin and Ch'u and
their leagues.[44] During the course of these years, Cheng
was forced to change its alignment many times. Table III
gives a general picture of the many changes involved.

TABLE III

General Slant of Cheng's Allegiance

	TO NORTH		TO SOUTH
Year	678-655	Year	655-653
B. C.	653-642	B. C.	642-627
	627-610		610-606
	605-599		599-586
	586-575		575-571
	571-565		565-560
	560-549		549-546

It might be supposed that such a situation left Cheng very little autonomy in the direction of its own affairs, but such was not the case. To begin with, neither Ch'u nor the allies of the Chou area could support an army in Cheng over an extended period.[45] Then too, the Cheng armies were sufficiently strong that they could usually withstand an attack until the current ally came to the rescue. Indeed, upon occasion the forces of Cheng were sufficiently strong to embark upon projects of their own for Cheng's expansion. In 607 B.C., Cheng not only took on the combined forces of Chin, Sung, Wei and Ch'en; but even defeated them in one engagement and captured 460 chariots.[46] Given its precarious position, however, autonomous actions by Cheng were perforce limited. In 565 B.C., when Cheng was allied, but not too closely, with Chin, it undertook an expedition against the small state of Ts'ai which was at that time a satellite of Ch'u. At that time Tzu-ch'an, while still a boy, showed his grasp of the current political situation by making a very accurate prediction of the results: "When the people of Ch'u come to punish us for this exploit, we must yield to their demands. Yielding to Ch'u, the army of Chin is sure to come upon us. Both Chin and Ch'u will attack Cheng which, within 4 or 5 years, will have no quiet."[47] During the course of its fluctuations between the camps of Ch'i or Chin and Ch'u the statesmen of Cheng seized every possible opportunity to improve the position of their own country. Occasionally Cheng transferred its allegiance quite voluntarily when it sensed that the other power was on the rise, so that it would not have to suffer the ravages of an attack directed against it. This was the case in 642 B.C., when there was internal strife in Ch'i following the death of Duke Huan. Cheng immediately transferred its loyalty to the Ch'u camp.[48]

Such a transfer of allegiance usually brought the armies of the former ally against Cheng. Following Cheng's transfer to the Ch'u camp in 642 B.C., the Chou states soon made a concerted effort under Duke Wen of Chin to win it back. When the opponent of Cheng's current ally attacked Cheng, the frequent procedure was for that ally to make a diversionary move into another state-- usually Ch'en or Sung--in order to force the withdrawal of pressure from Cheng. Such was the case in 604 B.C., when Ch'u invaded Cheng which currently owed allegiance

to the northern states. To relieve Cheng,Chin invaded
Ch'u's ally, Ch'en. Thus the state of Cheng, sometimes
knowingly, sometimes unwittingly, played the part of the
balancer. Perhaps its role is best termed that of a
"passive balancer." One important aspect of this balancing
process to which attention must be called is the almost
constant state of warfare in which it involved the Ch'un-
ch'iu states. There was constant insecurity and expectation of violence.

   If, however, as occasionally happened, this process,
which kept Ch'i or Chin and Ch'u at each other's throats
and which usually prevented the attainment of superiority,
did not seem to be working, there were other forces which
could be called into action. One of these was the state of
Ch'in which usually played the role of the "active balancer."
The Ch'un-ch'iu reports an invasion by Ch'in into Chin
territory in 615 B. C. A clue to the reason behind this is
given in the Tso-chuan report two years later of a
gathering of the states in Chin to celebrate the occurrence
of an insurrection in Ch'u and the defection to Chin of
some of the Ch'u states. The attack by Ch'in forced Chin
to guard its western borders and prevented it from taking
full advantage of Ch'u's distress. Fifteen years before
this, Ch'in had joined with Chin in attacking Ch'u and
Cheng, because it seemed that Ch'u had finally succeeded
in winning the complete loyalty of Cheng. Again in 589
B. C. , Ch'in aided Chin by applying pressure on Ch'u and
Cheng to desist from an invasion of Wei. Indeed, most of
the entries in the chronicle which concern themselves
with this distant western state, Ch'in, occur when, for a
short time, it steps into the picture to prevent either of
the leagues from gaining complete ascendancy. We do
know that there are no reports of any revolts within the
Ch'in territory, and we can only assume that during the
rest of the time it was consolidating gains in the west in
anticipation of the day when it could--and did--turn its
power toward that goal which it prevented its rivals from
attaining--the forceful conquest of what was to be China.[49]

   Starting in 568 B. C. , another power began to make
its influence felt. This was the state of Wu.[50] Its rise,
based in part upon the disaffection of some of the smaller
states in the East from Ch'u, parallels the decline in the
general power of Chin which was beginning to suffer under
the burdensome attempt to keep so large a territory under

control. Chin immediately turned to Wu as a natural ally
in its attempts to extinguish the threat of Ch'u power.
During the latter years of period VIII when it seemed
that Ch'u would definitely win the allegiance of the states
away from Chin, its ruler hastened to form an active
alliance with Wu--although the latter was supposedly a
rude and barbarian state. It was a case of calling in a
new world to redress the balance. Ch'u and its then firm
ally Cheng drove north to sever the communications between Chin and Wu, but failed. After 562 B. C. Ch'in was
forced to jump in on the side of Ch'u whose existence was
threatened by the combined attacks of Chin and Wu. There-
after, with the gradual decline in Chin power, Wu played the
part of counterpoise to Ch'u. Cheng was then relatively
free to follow its own interests. In 488 B. C., we find
Cheng hastening to the aid of Ts'ao which was being
attacked by Sung, feeling the threat of Sung superiority
among the northern states if Ts'ao fell, and not wanting
again to be caught between two powerful leagues. In such
a role, Cheng might once again be considered a fairly
important power in its own area. This rather extended
discussion of the balancing process in Ch'un-ch'iu times,
should serve to emphasize the importance of what we
have called the contextual component of state power.[51]

Now let us turn to a few more examples of the
assessments of state power which were made by the
statesmen of the Ch'un-ch'iu. We find from the many
statements recorded in the Tso-chuan that the leaders
not only were well aware of the process which was in
progress, but were also well able to make subtle calculations of their position. When, in 596 B. C., the Chin
ruler was cataloging the reasons why he felt secure, one
of his ministers pointed out to him how states strong in
such items as the horses and strategic outposts which he
had mentioned, had nevertheless fallen to other more
ambitious states. He added that the Chin ruler could not
even rely on the disunity then apparent in the government
of his opponents and pointed out that there had been a
rebellion in Ch'i immediately before Duke Huan had taken
over the reins of government. He urged the Duke of Chin
to persist in building up power and unity within his own
states.[52]

In fact, the Ch'un-ch'iu statesmen were so well aware
of the importance of internal unity and good leadership

that in 512 B. C. , when the ruler of Wu reformed his
government, a Lu official was convinced thereby of his
hostile intentions. He warned the Duke of Lu, "K'uang of
Wu has lately got that state, and is showing affection to
his people. He regards them as sons, and shares in all
their sufferings;--it must be with the intention of using
them."[53] Calculations on unity even played a part during
the conduct of hostilities. In 527 B. C. , when the Chin
officer Hsün Wu 荀吳 was attacking Hsien-yü 鮮虞 ,
some of the people revolted and offered to come over to
his side. He refused to have any dealings with the traitors,
pointing out that the loss of the future internal unity of the
state which he hoped to control would be greater than any
immediate gain.[54]   In 598 B. C. , after it had defeated the
state of Ch'i with some difficulty, Chin attempted to impose
a treaty requiring all the furrows in Ch'i's fields to run
from East to West so as to facilitate the passage of chariots in future operations; it was not too sure that its
control would continue to be decisive.[55]

There were few cases of planning for future action
vis-à-vis another state without a prior assessment of the
conditions in that state and especially of the extent to
which the government had the support of the people. On
this score the statesmen of Cheng were especially per-
ceptive. In 576 B. C. , the usual question came up as to
whether Cheng should be loyal to the cause of Chin or to
that of Ch'u. A Cheng minister pointed out regarding the
possible threat of the armies of Ch'u that there was dis-
content in their ranks because of the excesses of the
reigning Ch'u king. He said, "Let the king go on, aggra-
vating his offenses, till the people revolt from him. Without the people, who will fight for him?"[46] Ch'u itself
made fewer calculations of this type, and generally followed
a policy of taking what it could when it could, regardless
of future consequences. It is probable that it was for this
reason that it was the great power most consistently
plagued with disaffections among its allies. The policy
usually followed by Ch'u was voiced by its general Tzu-
fan 子反 in 576 B. C.: "When we can gain the advantage
over our enemies, we must advance without consideration
of covenants."[57]

There are several cases mentioned in the Tso-chuan
where one of the leaders of the time sums up a current
situation by pointing to two states either as natural allies

or natural enemies according to the circumstances, and advises action accordingly. Usually it was the nearest or the currently most threatening large power center which was being identified by another great power. An identification of the power centers at any particular moment makes more understandable the many changes and shifts of alignment carefully recorded in the Ch'un-ch'iu. Table IV lists the great powers of each of the twelve periods. For the table, characterization as a great power is based upon the following criteria: leadership of many states, great expansion of area of control, ability to engage another great power successfully in war, and identification as a major threat power by one of the statesmen of the time.

TABLE IV

Great Powers Of the Ch'un-ch'iu

PERIOD	1	2	3	4	5	6	7	8	9	10	11	12
Ch'u	x	x	x	x	x	x	x	x	x	x	x	x
Chin				x	x	x	x	x	x	x	x	
Ch'i		x	x	x		x			x	x		
Ch'in				x	x	x	x	x	x		x	
Wu							x	x	x	x	x	x
Cheng	x	x				x	x					
Sung		x			x							
Yüeh												x

As we have pointed out earlier, for the Ch'un-ch'iu to be a period of constant expansion and consolidation of state power would mean a growing intensity in the warfare among the power centers listed in Table IV. Here again the Lu chronicle and the Tso commentary give a consistent account of continuous growth. Perhaps a good clue to the increasing intensity of warfare is the number of chariots involved in various engagements. For every state which carried through the Ch'un-ch'iu there is a record of ever larger numbers. For example, in the case of Chin:

B. C.
632--700 chariots involved at the battle of Ch'eng-p'u 城濮
589--800 chariots contributed to allied campaign against Ch'i
541--1000 chariots added to its force
537--4900 chariots reported for the country
529--4000 chariots in a military display
501--1000 chariots at one border outpost

In the case of Ch'in, it is reported to have had about 300
chariots in the 650's B. C. , but by 530 B. C. we find over
1000 of its chariots engaged in battle. Chi's forces grew
from the first mention of 100 to over 4000 chariots by the
end of the Ch'un-ch'iu.[58]

The chronicle does not very often record the extent
of casualties in the battles, but from the tone of many of
the poems in the Classic of Poetry we may infer that
some of these battles were indeed violent. Tso does
report that of a special Ch'u raiding party of 3300 men
in a battle between Ch'u and Wu in 570 B. C. only 300 returned.[59] Starting with the battle of Ch'eng-p'u in 632
B. C. , the wars increased in intensity owing also to the fact
that they were fought between larger alliances on each
side.[60] Mei Ssu-p'ing further points out that the wars
lasted longer as the Spring and Autumn period went on.[61]
This would imply an increased economic cost of such
engagements and an augmented central power of the
governments sustaining them.

The greater intensity of warfare and of the suffering
which accompanied it resulted in a general peace movement culminating in a disarmament conference in 546
B. C.[62] This was a scheme of the Sung statesman Hsiang
Shu 向戌. His state, like Cheng, had frequently been the
arena of the battles between Ch'u and Chin. Hsiang went
to the various courts and proposed disarmament and the
establishment of a league of all the states as a means for
ending what seemed to be an almost constant state of war.
The states had, of course, at least to pretend an interest
in his idea. A Chin leader said, "War is destructive to
the people, an insect that eats up the resources of a State,
and the greatest calamity of the small States. If any one
try to put an end to it, though we think it cannot be done,
we must sanction his proposal. If we do not, Ch'u will do
so, and proceed to call the States together, so that we shall
lose the presidency of the covenants." The reaction in
Ch'u was similar. The Ch'i statesman involved observed
that he dared not refuse, since if the word got around that
he had refused to sanction the stoppage of wars, the people
in Ch'i might become disaffected. Hsiang's scheme was
accepted, and the leaders of fourteen large states
assembled in Sung that year for a conference. The important thing to note, however, is that the large states
based their acceptance of the proposal on their own

interests rather than on a general desire to do away with
arms.

At the meeting there was a great amount of haggling
about the text of the agreement, and when the wording was
finally determined, there was a dispute about whether
Chin or Ch'u should sign first. Ch'i and Ch'in did not
sign at all. The document contained only a general agreement for abolishing warfare, but it did provide that the
Ch'u satellites should appear regularly at the court of
Chin and the Chin satellites at the court of Ch'u. This
latter provision was the only part of the agreement which
worked for any time at all. Throughout the conference
there was an intense air of distrust; the Ch'u representatives even wore armor. Hsiang Shu felt that it had been
a great success and asked the ruler of Sung for a reward
for his part in it. Actually the conference was a total
failure from the point of view of its original objective.
The states went on their ways, distrusting each other
more than ever, and increasing their armaments.[63] The
prime minister of Sung was well aware that his colleague's
scheme had really contributed little, and his words to
Hsiang Shu when the latter presented him with the signed
text of the treaty deserve to be reproduced in full:

> 'It is by their arms that Chin and Ch'u keep the
> small States in awe. Standing in awe, the high
> and low in them are loving and harmonious; and
> through this love and harmony they can keep
> their States in quiet, and thereby serve the
> great States. In this is the way of preservation.
> If they were not kept in awe, they would become
> haughty. That haughtiness would produce
> disorder; that disorder would lead to their
> extinction. This is the way of ruin. Heaven has
> produced the five elements which supply men's
> requirements, and the people use them all. Not
> one of them can be dispensed with;--who can do
> away with the instruments of war? They have
> been long in requisition. It is by them that the
> lawless are kept in awe, and accomplished
> virtue is displayed. Sages have risen to their
> eminence by means of them; and men of
> confusion have been removed. The courses
> which lead to decline or to growth, to

preservation or to ruin, of blindness on one hand,
of intelligence on the other, are all traced to
these instruments; and you have been seeking to
do away with them:--is not your scheme a
delusion? No offence can be greater than to lead
the States astray by such a delusion. You have
escaped without punishment, and yet you have
sought for reward;--with an extreme insatiable-
ness.' With this he cut (to pieces the document)
and cast it away.[64]

The utopia of disarmament as a path to peace was
no answer in Ch'un-ch'iu times. Not only were the states
of Ch'i and Ch'in not included in the agreement, but there
was no method to prevent the state of Wu, which was
gaining power in the east, from using arms against the
other states. The prior conditions of trust and agreement
among all the states had not been met. And who could
anticipate when some shift in the components of power of
one of the states would create new feelings of insecurity
which would dispel even such trust and agreement as had
previously been achieved?

Chapter V

LEADERSHIP IN ANCIENT CHINA

The effective role of the components of state power was naturally determined by the leadership ability of the individuals who directed state policies in Chou times. It is relatively difficult to dig beneath the surface and determine just what was the pattern of life in Ancient China. How, precisely, were political decisions carried into force? What were the general effects thereof upon the masses who, as one writer has put it, ranked "just one step above the royal herds?"[1] It should be obvious from our previous discussion that oligarchy was the form of government within the various states.[2] It is mainly about the élites at the top of a very broad pyramid that written sources report. This is understandable, since only members of the ruling élites had the opportunity to become literate. Their monopoly of the learning of the time insured a dominant reflection of their interests and actions in the writings which have come down to us. Some of the modern Chinese writers, and especially those with Communist leanings, have been investigating the life of the common people in those times.[3] But as long as we have to depend mainly upon written sources, a more specific knowledge of political life in the Ch'un-ch'iu period will be limited to those groups which occupied positions of influence.

A good example of this limitation is the fact, noted above, that the Tso-chuan gives very few reports of the casualties among the troops which accompanied the chariots of the leaders. Tso reports that in a battle in 707 B. C., between the Chou king and his allies and the state of Cheng a wound was suffered by the king. This was obviously a hard fought battle, and yet that is the only casualty reported.[4] Again in 578 B. C., in a battle between Chin, Ch'i, Sung, Wei, Ts'ao, Lu, Chu, and T'eng against Ch'in the only casualty reported is the death of the ruler of Ts'ao. [5]

Since it was these élite groups which in the main determined the course of events during the Ch'un-ch'iu,
this limitation of our knowledge is not too important. It
is necessary for us to analyze the shifts in the composition of these ruling élites, and our sources are adequate
for this. On this score, we have already noted that the
Ch'un-ch'iu was in general a period of important change.
There was a shift of control from noble feudal families to
an increasing number of functionaries in the various states.
This shift on one hand was aided by, and on the other contributed to, some of the other changes which we have noted
above. For example, the process of state expansion and
the consolidation of state power called for the creation of
new administrative offices. The filling of these offices
with a new type of official contributed to the expansion and
consolidation of state power. In the same way, the growing
complexity of social organization within the Ch'un-ch'iu
states was paralleled by a growing complexity in the administrative organization.[6] This was the period of the
real beginning of the Chinese bureaucratic state.

In examining the shift of control away from the feudal
élite, it is impossible to achieve easy generalizations. In
some states, such as Lu, the various feudal clans took over
the administrative posts; and as a result, the position of
the ruling house was weakened. In other states the new
officials rallied to the cause of the ruling family and the
other noble families faded into the background. This was
what happened in Ch'i. In still other cases there was no
radical change from the original feudal order so that the
position of the state continued to depend in great measure
upon the character of the current ruler.

In most cases the transfer of political control from
a feudal aristocracy to a growing bureaucracy was a slow
process. It depended upon other developments such as the
economic improvement necessary to support the growing
officialdom, state expansion, and so forth. One indication
of the slowness of change is that in several cases the new
administrative offices of the states became hereditary. [7]
The new officials found many occasions for increasing the
scope of their political power. For example, at the death
of one of the rulers they could carry on state functions
until the next ruler came to the throne. In 685 B. C., following the Ch'i ruler's death, the Duke of Lu met a minister of that state and signed a treaty with him. [8] Again, the

ruler of a large state frequently had to authorize a minister to deal with the heads of the smaller states while he
was himself dealing with a state of size equal to his own.
It was also common during the early years for the ministers to assume a more active role in internal government,
while the rulers themselves carried on external diplomacy,
the demand for which was constantly increasing. Finally,
in giving advice to rulers, the more practical class of
officials began to replace the diviners. [9]

The growing "bureaucracy" was also encouraged by
the increased importance of the symbol of the state. We
have pointed above to the increasing patriotism. In many
cases where the ruler remained strong, he himself became identified with the state. In general, however, by
the closing years of the Ch'un-ch'iu period, the symbol
of the state had assumed a more important place than the
ruler. In 582 B. C., for example, while their ruler was
being held a prisoner in Chin, to show that they could
carry on without him, the people of Cheng besieged the
little state of Hsü 許.[10] Again, the state of Lu was directed
from 517 to 510 B. C., by the Chi 季 family while the ruler,
Duke Chao 昭公, was a fugitive outside his state.[11] This
latter case was in one respect exceptional. The vassal
families in Lu probably continued strong because of the
close relationship of Lu to the Chou system. In most of
the states the growing power of the officials was at the
expense of these feudal families.[12] As pointed out above,
the elimination of their power was one of the first targets
of Kuan-tzu's reforms.

All this in turn necessitated and aided the change from
the old feudal rules of conduct, li 禮, to a more formal
legal system, fa 法. The new class of ministers needed
new rules to buttress its continued existence. Thus, for
example, by 597 B. C., it was possible in several states
for officers to sign treaties. Under the old feudal rules,
this was entirely improper, wu li 無禮. In 535 B. C.,
K'ung Ch'eng-tzu 孔成子, a minister of the state of Wei,
was able to determine the successor to his former ruler.[13]
Under the old feudal rules this decision had rested entirely
with the members of the royal house.

The Ch'un-ch'iu reports very faithfully on this growing
weight of the "bureaucracy" in the various states. Figure
I presents this shift in graphic form. By noting in every
other one of our twenty-year periods the personages

involved in the interstate meetings (hui 會) as recorded
in the Lu annals, whether rulers only, rulers and ministers, or ministers only, we can chart the shift very clearly. The importance of this trend is doubly emphasized
when we recall that the Ch'un-ch'iu presents the court
records and should perforce be mainly concerned with
the rulers.

It is relevant to point out that the heroes--the men
whose names have been familiar to Chinese ears through
history-- of the first years of the Ch'un-ch'iu are rulers,
whereas those of the later years are ministers and advisors. The exception is, of course, Kuan-tzu, but we
have already pointed out his role in anticipating and pre-
cipitating the very changes in point. Moreover, Duke
Huan has been regarded as every bit as much a hero as
his famous advisor.[14] Mencius reports that the king of

Figure I

Growing Importance of Officers in CH'UN-CH'IU
on the Basis of Meetings (Hui 會)*

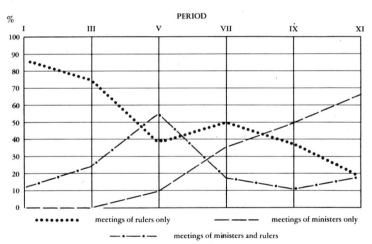

(*The word Hui 會 as used in the Ch'un-ch'iu indicates two general types of meetings; one a
joining for the purpose of some combined action,
the other a formal meeting for deliberation on
some problem. Both are included in the above
figures.)

Ch'i inquired very eagerly of him about the administration of Duke Huan.[15] The logical sequel can be found in
the pages of the work attributed to Lü Pu-wei呂不偉 , the
famous statesman of the Warring Kingdoms era. He argues that for a ruler to become famous he must first have
top flight ministers.[16] By his time the importance of
officers and advisors had generally eclipsed that of the
rulers.

We can in general say then that by the close of the
Ch'un-ch'iu period, most of the members of the feudal
aristocracy were fulfilling merely ceremonial functions.[17]
They were completely outnumbered by the growing body
of functionaries, and were of constantly diminishing
importance in the effective direction of affairs. Moreover,
they were increasingly unable to match the growing influence of the merchants who were filtering into administrative posts. [18] The whole development was a logical
cause of, and accompaniment to, the decline of the early
Chou feudal institutions.

What then were the types of leadership for both
officials and feudal aristocracy, and how did they influence the course of events? Let us begin with the hereditary rulers of the various states. We can divide them
roughly into two classes. The great majority preferred
to sit back and enjoy life and did not care to enter actively
into the growing role which their positions made possible.
They tried, however, to assure the perpetuation of their
families and their final authority to rule. On these interests was based the complex system of intermarriage
among the various ruling houses. A marriage alliance
was calculated not only to bring outside aid in case possession of the throne were endangered, but also to
increase state power. Thus, in 672 B.C., 623 B.C., and
again in 604 B.C., we find Lu making marriage alliances
with her more powerful neighbor Ch'i. At the same time
Lu allied herself by marriage to the states of Chü and
Chi in 667 B.C., and again in 615 B.C.[19] In case the
ruling family of a particular state was forced out of
power, its various members took refuge in several states
so that the family's total elimination would be less likely. [20]

Occasionally, a second type of ruler, one with a real
feeling for his position, would come into power; and, if
he had the proper personality and ability, the backing of
the masses reinforcing his ceremonial position would give

him great opportunity for accomplishment. Such, for example, was the young ruler who came to power in the
state of Chin in 573 B. C. He was but fourteen years old
at the time, but he showed a real feeling for command.
Tso reports that when the ministers of Chin offered him
the throne, he said "When men seek a ruler, it is to have
one who shall give out orders. If, when they have called
him to the head of the State, they do not follow his orders,
what use have they for him? If you mean to obey me, say
so today; if not, say so today."[21] The officers agreed to
follow him and made a written agreement with him to
that effect. This ruler, Duke Tao 悼公 went on to reor-
ganize and revitalize the government. Tso continues,
"No word of dissatisfaction or reviling was heard among
the people, and thus, the place of Chin as leader of the
other States was restored."[22] Duke Tao was a charismatic
leader, one with an innate ability to rule, who stimulated
those under him and in turn was stimulated by them, and
who commanded unswerving loyalty.

The charismatic leader par excellence of the Ch'un-
ch'iu was Duke Wen of Chin. Let us discuss him in some
detail as a case study. [23] He was born Ch'ung-erh 重耳 ,
the third son of the Duke of Chin. While still quite young,
he was forced to flee from his state when his two elder
brothers were killed so that a younger brother might be
put on the throne. Before taking over the rule of Chin he
wandered from state to state for nineteen years, a period
of exile which gave him important acquaintances and experiences. He visited most of the leading courts of his
day. It was apparent to some of the rulers of the other
states that here was a man with great personal magnetism,
and one to whom, obviously, "heaven was opening the
way." His hosts during his exile were impressed not only
with his personality, but also by the number and quality
of loyal followers who accompanied him through all these
years. For example, while he was a guest in Ts'ao, the
wife of a minister of that state said, "When I look at the
followers of the prince of Chin, every one of them is fit
to be chief minister of a State."[24] The Sung minister Shu-
chan 叔詹 was equally impressed by the calibre of Ch'ung-
erh's followers.

During his exile he proved himself also to be politically quite astute. His hosts made all sorts of predictions
about his success if he should return to the throne in his

state. Referring to Ch'ung-erh and his followers Tso
reports, "When they came to Ch'u, the viscount was one
day feasting the prince, and said, 'If you return to Chin,
and become its marquis, how will you recompense my
kindness to you?' The prince replied, 'Women, gems,
and silks, your lordship has, feathers, hair, ivory and
hides, are all produced in your lordship's country; those
of them that come to Chin are but your superabundance.
What should I have with which to recompense your kindness?' "[25] Duke Wen not only showed his appreciation of
Ch'u's economic strength but also managed to avoid future
obligations binding on his state when he should return.

After he had returned to Chin and secured the throne,
he proved an able administrator. He revamped the military
organization of the state, and like Kuan-tzu in Ch'i, made
it the core of his civil administration.[26] He it was who
led the Chou states in the battle of Ch'eng-p'u in 632 B. C.
The Chou states were perhaps more at one under his
leadership than at any other time. His officers admired
him not only for his ability to lead but also for the high
moral standards which he set. During his reign, 636 to
628 B. C., Chin absorbed many new territories. Most of
them were happy to come under Duke Wen's rule. Tso
reports that in 635 B. C., Duke Wen refused to break his
word in order to add the state of Yüan原 to his domain.
He said, "Good faith is the precious jewel of a State, and
what the people depend upon. If I get Yüan and lose my
good faith, of what protection could the people be assured?
My loss would be greater than my gain."[27] Later, the
people of Yüan came and offered him their state in such a
way that he could accept it. Such a man, who kept his
word in preference to adding to his territory, was rare in
the Ch'un-ch'iu, and this characteristic of Ch'ung-erh proved
a great asset. Although his rule was a very short one, the
institutions which he created, and Chin's leadership of the
Chou states, lasted through most of the remainder of the
Ch'un-ch'iu period.

Not all the rulers who enjoyed the position of command
achieved the popularity of the famous Duke Wen. The
rulers of Ch'u and Ch'in were, in general, rougher types
than those of the other states. Some were less able than
others, but almost all possessed the charismatic gift of
ability to command. In 545 B. C., for example, the Cheng
diplomat Tzu-t'ai-shu 子太叔 reported back from a

mission to Ch'u. He said of the Ch'u ruler, "Instead of
cultivating his government and his virtue, he is blindly
eager to command the States, and so gratify his ambition."[28] Four years later the Cheng diplomat Yu-chi
游吉 reported about the successor of this king, "The
extravagance of the king of Ch'u is excessive, and he is
delighted with his position. He is sure to call the States
together. We shall be going there in no time."[29] Such
rulers, however, do not appear very frequently in Ch'un-
ch'iu times. Most of the rulers of the various states had
to rely on their ministers and generals, while they occupied themselves with their harems and other pleasures.

We can distinguish also between two general types of
ministers. One type openly assumed the active direction
of the affairs of state and practically took over the re-
sponsibilities of the ruler, who was then forced into a
purely ceremonial position. This type of officer displayed
many of the characteristics of a charismatic leader. He
enjoyed his position and accepted the responsibility which
it carried. The second type was the more traditional
bureaucrat who preferred to carry on his administration
behind the façade of the royal house. His position was
mainly that of an advisor, but if he had a sufficiently
strong personality, his advice usually became the rule of
the land. Most of the growing body of functionaries were
weaker combinations of these two types. We are interested,
however, in those leaders who were sufficiently important
in the direction of affairs to influence effectively the course
of events, and these were usually one or the other of the
two main types. Let us examine the role of a minister of
each type in Ch'un-ch'iu times.

Kung-sun Ch'iao 公孫僑 , or as he is better known,
Tzu-ch'an 子產 , was one of the most famous statesmen
of the whole Ch'un-ch'iu period.[30] From 554 B. C. until
his death in 522 B. C., he held high offices in Cheng, a
state whose unique position we have already discussed.
He was in active control of the state from 543 B. C., and
throughout his administration he became increasingly
popular. By the time of his death his fame had spread to
all the other states. It is reported that Confucius himself
wept for him like a brother, and that the people of his
own state "mourned for him as if they had lost a close
relative."[31] We have pointed out above that he had a
realistic appreciation of the interstate politics of his

time, and knew that he must make his own state strong if
it were to survive. So effective was his administration,
that for a while it seemed Cheng would become one of the
great powers of his day. In fact, it is reported that Shu
Hsiang 叔向), the chief minister of Chin, advised his ruler
that Cheng could not profitably be attacked as long as
Tzu-ch'an was in control there. [32] The stories told about
Tzu-ch'an leave no doubt that he was the real ruler of
Cheng and that he was so recognized by the people. Except
as noted in the traditional genealogies, we are hardly
aware of the names of the rulers of the royal house whom
he served.

Tzu-ch'an had his own theory of how a state should
be administered, and he kept to it closely and conscien-
tiously. When he was first asked to assume the government of the state he declined, pointing out that Cheng was
small, the influence of the clans was still quite strong,
many favorites were in positions of influence, and that
the neighboring states were sure to make trouble. He
agreed to assume the administration only after he had
been promised a free hand. [33] The changes which he then
quite suddenly introduced were aimed at a "centralized
unification of power and of social customs." [34] "Tzu-ch'an
made the central cities and border lands of the State
be exactly defined, and enjoined on the high and inferior
officers to wear (only) their distinctive robes. The fields
were all marked out by their banks and ditches. The
houses and fields, ching 井 , were divided into fives,
responsible to one another. The great officers, who were
faithful and temperate, were advanced to higher dignities,
while the extravagant were punished and taken off." [35] To
this account of Tzu-ch'an's early administrative changes
Tso adds the following:

"When the government had been in Tzu-ch'an's hands
one year, all men sang of him,

'We must take our clothes and caps, and hide
    them all away;
We must count our fields by fives, and own
    a mutual sway.
We'll gladly join with him who this Tzu-ch'an
    will slay. '

But in three years the song was,

'Tis Tzu-ch'an who our children trains;
    Our fields to Tzu-ch'an owe their gains.
    Did Tzu-ch'an die, who'd take the reins?' "36

Five years later, the security of the state of Cheng
called for even more stringent measures on the part of
the central administration. Tzu-ch'an lost no time in
issuing a decree for carrying them out,

on which the people of the State reviled him,
saying, 'His father died on the road, and he
himself is a scorpion's tail. Issuing such
orders for the State, what will the State do
under them?' Tzu-k'uan [子寬] reported these
remarks to Tzu-ch'an who said, 'there is no
harm in it. If it only benefit the altars, I will
live or die. Moreover, I have heard that when
a good-doer does not change his measures, he
can calculate on success. The people are not
to be gratified in this; the measure must not
be altered. The ode [a lost ode] says,

'If one's rules and righteousness be not
    in error,
Why regard the words of people.'

I will not change it. 37

We also know that Tzu-ch'an gave himself whole-
heartedly to his work. "Government," he said, "is like
the work of husbandry. You must think of it day and night,
thinking of what is to be done first, and how the end is to
be accomplished. Then labor at it morning and evening;
but in what you do, do not go beyond what you have thought
over; just as the husbandmen keep within the dividing
banks. In this way you will commit few errors."38
    On most of his policies Tzu-ch'an sought the advice
of other capable officials. He was famous as an orator
and put much effort into the composition of his speeches.
When he felt that they were satisfactory, he then repeated
them for other Cheng officials and before delivering them
incorporated their suggestions. This was especially true
of the effective speeches which he delivered at diplomatic
gatherings.39 It was by oratorical and diplomatic ability

that in 523 B. C., he prevented Chin from interfering in
the internal affairs of Cheng.[40] He was careful in his
choice of administrators and paid close attention to popular opinion on their work. It is reported that once when a
man was seized for criticizing the government, some of
the officials wanted to have him put to death. Tzu-ch'an
refused, saying ". . . our best plan is to hear what is
said, and use it as medicine."[41]

That Tzu-ch'an is a good representative of the different institutional tone of the later years of the Ch'un-ch'iu,
is borne out in one of the most interesting stories in the
Tso-chuan. In 536 B. C., under the direction of Tzu-ch'an,
tripods were cast in Cheng. On them was engraved a new
legal code, with specification of various crimes and their
punishments. This caused Shu Hsiang, the more conserva-
tive minister of Chin and an admirer of Tzu-ch'an, to
write him a rather bitter letter of disapproval.[42] He
wrote, "At first I considered you [as my model], but
now I have ceased to do so--when the people know what
the exact laws are, they do not stand in awe of their
superiors.... When once the people know the grounds for
contention, they will cast propriety away, and make their
appeals to your descriptions. They will all be contending
about a matter as small as the point of an awl or a knife."
He went on to predict disaster and accused Tzu-ch'an of
flagrantly ignoring future consequences. Tzu-ch'an replied, "As to what you say, I have not the talents nor the
ability to act for posterity; my object is to save the present
age. I cannot accept your instructions, but I dare not for-
get your great kindness."[43] According to the modern
German sinologue Hellmut Wilhelm, Tzu-ch'an realized
that he was living in a different age and could not be
concerned with the shadows of the feudal past.[44] There
seems to be no doubt that he had the complete support of
the people of Cheng and that he enjoyed a position of full
authority there throughout his life.

The other type of minister, who preferred to act in
the name of his ruler, is perhaps best exemplified by one
of Tzu-ch'an's contemporaries, the statesman of Ch'i,
Yen-tzu 晏子 (also Yen Ying 晏嬰 and Yen P'ing-chung
晏平仲). [45] Yen-tzu is famous as an advisor for three
successive rulers in Ch'i, and he is equally famous in
Chinese legend as a clever diplomat who managed to keep
the prestige of his state high in the courts which he visited.

He was very apt in turning a phrase to his own advantage and used this ability to persuade his princes to accept many reforms which he desired. Most of our information about Yen-tzu is contained in the many accounts of his conversations with his several rulers.

He was one of the first statesmen of the time to realize that the people were becoming restless under the constant pressure of interstate conflict, and he consistently urged measures which would lighten their load. Yen-tzu warned that the best way toward security lay in the support of the people. "The people first and then yourself" (Hsien-min erh-hou shen 先民而後身) was the principle which he enjoined upon his ruler.[46] Under his direction, but on the orders of the prince of Ch'i, many internal reforms were carried out. Laws were made less harsh, taxes were lightened, and measures were enacted for taking care of the poor and feeble.[47] Although Yen-tzu was popular with the people, and they realized that he was responsible for their improved lot, he kept himself in the background and refused many of the honors which the Dukes of Ch'i wished to bestow upon him.[48] Like Tzu-ch'an, he was greatly admired by his younger contemporary, Confucius.[49] The great historian Ssu-ma Ch'ien has only the highest words of praise for him.[50]

Two other groups held positions of prominence in the ruling élites of Ch'un-ch'iu times. The first of these, the families of the vassals within the states, we have already mentioned. Except in some of the Chou states where the remains of feudalism continued fairly strong, their position was one of declining importance, as we have already indicated. We need not concern ourselves with them here.

The other group consisted of scholars and philosophers who, during the closing years of the Ch'un-ch'iu, were beginning to have some influence in determining state policies. Occasionally these men played active roles in the administration, but their usual role was to give advice, based upon the lofty principles which they expounded. For the most part their words went unheeded, lacking direct relationship to the political exigencies of the day. Such, for example, was the role of Confucius. It is unfortunate that the men of action--Tzu-ch'an, Yen-tzu, Shu Hsiang, and the others--did not have the leisure to record their own more pragmatic philosophies. Because of the scarcity of reliable sources, our reconstructions can be flimsy at best. Thus the political philosophies of the Ch'un-ch'iu which have come down to us were written by the scholars who had time for literary endeavors but who lacked much practical knowledge of political realities.[51]

This, in general, was the status of the leadership in the Ch'un-ch'iu period. Undoubtedly the greatest strides in state expansion were made under the charismatic rulers and ministers. The more conventional or bureaucratic ministers were more concerned with making their states secure through internal consolidation of central power. A good example is found in the relationship of Yen-tzu with the second ruler whom he served. This was Duke Chuang 莊公 of Ch'i who ruled that state from 552 to 547 B. C. We find Yen-tzu reproaching Duke Chuang for thinking only of enlarging Ch'i, and for admiring only raw power. He urged the duke to consolidate his position at home and to win the hearts of his people. The duke would not listen to him and undertook more campaigns, even daring to attack Chin, the powerful leader of the Chou states. [52] Occasionally a popular figure, such as Tzu-ch'an, could combine internal consolidation with external expansion, but such men were few. To most of the active leaders among the princes, such as Duke Chuang of Ch'i and many of the kings of Ch'u, self-fulfillment came in military leadership. The enterprises of these men were the direct cause of many of the wars recorded in the Lu chronicles. But we must remember that they also produced some major improvements. They brought increasing contacts and cultural development through interchange of ideas; they encouraged the development of better communications facilities; and they defined ever larger areas for increasing administrative experience, without which the eventual unification of China would have been impossible.

A final word must be added about the role of the peasants, the masses of the Spring and Autumn times. We have already pointed out that their role was for the most part passive. Yet, since in any undertaking they were the group which had to be led, they occasionally set limits beyond which the rulers and ministers could not go. Their enthusiasm for a cause determined their fighting strength, and we have pointed out above how important it was to realize this fact.

Once in a great while the people revolted and refused to continue under a ruler who had been excessively harsh or ambitious. In 613 B. C., for example, the people of the little state of Chu 莒 expelled their ruler, and even a force of 800 chariots, supplied by the Chou states who supported his right to his throne, could not succeed in keeping him there. A compromise had to be made with the people on another ruler. Again, in 620 B. C., the people of Chin were unwilling to have the son of the wife from Ch'in, the rival state of the time, come to the throne. Another son was picked even at the risk of war with Ch'in. [54] We have seen that in one case the Marquis of Wei even went so far as to sound out the loyalty of his people in an open audience, before he determined to leave the Chou league which was then under Chin's direction. [55] These are a few examples reported by Tso where the will of the masses did play at least a limited role. When loyally behind the administration, they could make even a small state powerful.

In general, we can say, that in leadership as in other fields, the free sources give a faithful picture of consistent change. The officials who were replacing the feudal élite not only were themselves an evidence of this change, but they also were greatly responsible for many of the other changes which we have noted in other aspects of life in the Ch'un-ch'iu period.

Chapter VI

INTERSTATE RELATIONS

Let us turn now in somewhat more detail to the actual
conduct of relations among the Ch'un-ch'iu states. It was
to be expected that certain patterns should develop for the
carrying on of these relations. Such patterns created a
greater ease in maintaining the relations, and facilitated
the flow of trade and information. There were advantages
involved for every state which adhered to the pattern, a
mutual benefit to be derived for all--up to a certain point.
These patterns naturally created certain uniformities
which are fairly easy to discern, and these uniformities
taken as a whole constituted a system of state behavior
expectations which enabled a state to make at least a
rough assessment of its situation at any particular time
and to forecast the consequences of its actions with a fair
degree of accuracy.

These uniformities in interstate relations during the
Ch'un-ch'iu have been most intensively studied. From
Han times the Chinese traditionalists fastened upon some
of these uniformities as a further proof of the unity under
the Chou empire. This led to their preoccupation with the
morality of the actions of the various Ch'un-ch'iu states,
rather than with an analysis of the rationale of state actions.
Thus, for example, the greater part of the Kung-yang and
Ku-liang commentaries upon the Ch'un-ch'iu chronicle is
concerned with whether or not the events recorded fit in
with the elaborate system of rules which supposedly
existed under the Chou Empire. The three ritual works
in the Chinese Classics, the Li-chi禮記, the I-li儀禮,
and the Chou-li周禮, set up an elaborate system of
administration, ceremonies, ranks of officials, methods
of intercourse, and behavior standards which also supposedly formed the model for the Chou Empire. While
these works may have had some basis in reality under
the early Chou, they are now generally conceded to be,
in the main, later fabrications. [1]

Some modern Chinese scholars have studied the uniformities in state behavior during the Ch'un-ch'iu under the title of "Interstate Law of Ancient China," and indeed there is little reason for us to doubt that the patterns of interstate intercourse which developed did constitute a rudimentary system of interstate law.[2] Yet it must be pointed out that most of these modern students have been none too careful in their utilization of the early sources, drawing without hesitation on such works as the Chou-li to prove their points. There can be little doubt, as we have pointed out above, that the bald chronicles and unsystematizing pre-Han texts constitute the most reliable basis upon which to reconstitute the system of interstate law as it developed in Ancient China.[3]

The patterns of interstate intercourse during the Ch'un-ch'iu did to some extent originate in the feudalism which existed in a limited area under the Western Chou. There were, however, other sources of equal importance. There was a growing body of custom which developed as contacts and commerce increased; there were the increasing number of treaties which were signed during the period and to which appeal was frequently made; and there were the patterns and rules set up within the leagues of states. In one of the recent works on the interstate law Hung Chün-p'ei states his belief that "The greater part of the interstate law of the Ch'un-ch'iu period was produced in the league headed by Chin."[4]

It is, of course, necessary, in our discussion of the multi-state system of the Spring and Autumn times, to take account of this system of interstate law which developed. We are, however, less interested in the formal aspect--the listing of the many rules and forms--than in the effectiveness of the law. When did the states adhere to the pattern, when did they not, and why? It is perhaps typical of most of the students of the interstate law of the Ch'un-ch'iu that they have ignored these questions. In their eagerness to find and catalogue the various rules they have failed to realize that those cases where the rules did not hold were probably of greater significance. Thus, for example, Dr. Ch'en Shih-ts'ai points out a general rule to the effect that a state should not conquer another state whose ruler had the same surname, and adds that on this score all three of the commentaries to the Ch'un-ch'iu condemn Wei's 衛 conquest of Hsing 邢

in 635 B. C.[5] We are more interested in the reasons why
Wei, a relatively small state, should ignore a commonly
accepted canon at this time at the risk of general distrust
and ill will on the part of those states which accepted it.
The Ch'un-ch'iu and Tso-chuan report other actions by
Wei at this time to increase its power and consolidate its
position, including an alliance with Lu. This undoubtedly
was because of the growing threat of the superior power
of Chin under the inspired leadership of Duke Wen. Wei's
actions in this case were of little use, for Chin did
temporarily take over the state in 632 B. C. to safeguard
its flank in preparing for the battle of Ch'eng-p'u.[6] At the
time of its action in 635 B. C., however, Wei felt that the
absorption of Hsing offered a better guarantee of its
security than adherence to an otherwise generally accepted
rule. But let us turn to a more general consideration of
some of these laws of interstate behavior.

A great many of the canons of interstate law in the
Ch'un-ch'iu concerned diplomacy among the states --
diplomacy in the more narrow sense of the term: the
actual conduct of relations. We have seen that with the
exception of the states which from time to time assumed
the role of leaders in their various areas, the states, in
general, dealt with each other on a footing of equality.[7]
Within a few years after the beginning of the Ch'un-ch'iu
the ranks of the rulers of the various states as derived
from the former feudal system were without any practical
significance.[8] Diplomacy and the fruits which it bore such
as alliances, treaties, and economic aid, were in the
main dictated by the security interests of the states rather
than by former feudal rank. The free Chinese sources
record the various diplomatic activities under such terms
as ch'ao 朝 , a court visit paid by one ruler to another;
hui 會 , meetings of officials or nobles of different states;
p'in 聘 , missions of friendly inquiries sent by the ruler
of one state to another; shih 使 , emissaries sent from
one state to another; shou 狩 , hunting parties where the
representatives of different states combined business
with pleasure, etc. Such activities are recorded with
increasing frequency by the Ch'un-ch'iu and Tso-chuan;
this, of course, was a logical consequence of the increasing area of contact.

A realization had developed by Ch'un-ch'iu times
that the continued existence of a state depended quite as

much upon its external policies--its ability to attract
allies, to pick the winning side, etc. -- as on its internal
strength. The group of officials whose duties involved
relations with other states became ever larger and more
complex within the more powerful states.[9] In the early
years of the Ch'un-ch'iu, the rulers of the various states
were the most important personages in the conduct of
external affairs. They soon came to rely on their hsing-
jen 行人 or messengers to carry on most of the preliminary work in any matters of importance. These hsing-
jen were usually officials of fairly high rank within the
state who carried out these commissions on a temporary
basis. There were also the ambassadors, shih 使, who
carried out more and more of the ceremonial duties of
the ruler outside his state. During the first half of the
Spring and Autumn period the rulers themselves usually
had to be present at the signing of any agreements which
committed their states to any action.

A most interesting perceptible trend in the conduct
of external affairs in Ancient China was the changing role
played by the hsiang 相 or prime ministers--perhaps
"chancellor" is a better translation of the term. We have
noted that these officers increasingly directed the affairs
of the states, usually in the name of the rulers. At first
their attention was directed toward the internal consolidation of state power and the elimination of the power of the
powerful hereditary families within the states. As time
went on, however, they also came to realize the importance
of external alignment in determining the strength not only
of their states but also of their positions. They, therefore,
assumed an ever more active role in diplomacy. As it
became more apparent that a struggle for state survival
was in progress, their attention and time were turned
almost exclusively outside the borders of their own states.
An indication not only of the growing power of the hsiang
but of their concern with external affairs was the fact that
the prime ministers of several states were able to, and
did with great haste, repudiate a convenant which had
been signed in 506 B. C. by the rulers of their various
states. The covenant, based mainly on dynastic interests,
cut across traditional alliance patterns and threatened to
upset the security policies on which the ministers had
been working.[10] The culmination of this trend was reached
later in Chan-kuo times when the pattern of the struggle

for the control of the whole China area is even more clearly
perceptible. By that time, the conduct of external affairs
and the establishment of an external policy for security
had become almost the exclusive concern of the prime
ministers.[11]

In an age and culture where ceremonies played an
extremely important part in everyday life, it was to be
expected that there should be a great amount of ritual in
the relations between the states. Although the greater
part of the content of the three ritual classics is now conceded to be the work of later writers, when read in con-
junction with the other free pre-Han texts, they do at
least give some indication of the importance of the ceremonial aspect of interstate life. The I-li, for example,
lays down many formal rules for the ceremonies for the
reception of a mission from another state, including the
manner in which the officials are to be housed and even
the number of dishes to be served at the banquet given
for them by the ruler of the state to which they were
sent.[12] Tso confirms many of these ceremonial aspects
as reported in the I-li but not in such meticulous detail.[13]
Many of the ceremonies were derived from the former
feudalism, others developed with the increasing contacts.
What is important from our point of view is that the states
strove to outdo each other in their ceremonies to such an
extent that their ability to put on a rich ceremonial front
frequently determined their position among their associates.

Such a determination was not entirely without a practical basis for at least two reasons. In the first place,
the extent to which elaborate ceremonies could be carried
on for visiting dignitaries depended in large measure upon
the economic strength of the state. Large outlays were
required even to the extent of erecting special houses for
the envoys.[14] Secondly, since the rigidity of ceremonial
forms required a great amount of discipline, their observation provided an indication of the efficiency of the current
regime. The Yen-tzu Ch'un-ch'iu reports that "Duke
P'ing 平 of Chin wanted to invade Ch'i and sent Fan
Chao 范昭 to investigate the political situation there."
Fan Chao, pretending to be drunk, attempted in various
ways to have Yen-tzu and other officials act contrary to
the ceremonies, but did not succeed. On this basis he
reported back to Duke P'ing that Ch'i could not at that

time be successfully invaded.[15]

The accent on ceremonies led to an extreme formality
in diplomatic relations. Each emissary had to go through
a rigid pattern in presenting to the ruler of the state where
he had been sent, his proper credentials, chieh 節 . He
could not accept any gifts for himself, he must not accept
any ceremonies to which his rank did not entitle him, and
he must conduct himself at all times in a very formal
manner. The envoys also had to be able to respond in
proper manner to the toasts given at the banquets in their
honor. This usually involved the ability to select for the
occasion a fitting verse from the well known songs of the
time. Tso reports in many places the precise verses re-
cited by the various diplomats at these banquets.[16]

Although there were no permanent legations maintained in Ch'un-ch'iu times, the frequency of diplomatic
intercourse even from the earliest years provided almost
the equivalent.[17] The ceremonies accorded to an envoy
made it necessary for him to remain for quite a period
of time, and the number of occasions which required the
sending of a mission led even to overlapping.[18] For the
purposes of our discussion here, the reasons for diplomatic activity might be listed under the following headings:
dynastic, economic, security, and legal; the categories
are by no means exclusive.

Practically all the major events in the life of a ruling
family required some sort of diplomatic representation
from the other friendly states. The assumption of the
throne, burial of the former ruler six months after his
death, marriage of a ruler to a daughter of another ruler:
all these events brought, for ceremonial purposes at
least, gatherings of diplomatic representatives at the
court in question. On these occasions, when the proper
ceremonies had been dispensed with, interstate affairs
were frequently discussed and settled. Most of the earlier
entries in the Confucian chronicle are concerned with
activities of this nature. These missions in turn required
missions of acknowledgment, so that each of the dynastic
reasons for diplomatic activity usually required at least
two missions. For example, many representatives of
friendly states were present in Lu when Duke Wen assumed
the throne in 626 B. C. The Ch'un-ch'iu also records that
year a mission of friendly inquiries from Lu to Ch'i. Tso
in commenting on this entry states the general rule that

on "the accession of princes of States, their ministers should go everywhere on such friendly missions, main- taining and cultivating old friendships, and forming external alliances of support."[19] Likewise, the various rulers sent envoys to commiserate with friendly sover- eigns whose lands were suffering the misfortunes of flood, drought, fire or famine; and again to participate in such joyous occasions as the building of a new palace, a new capital or a like venture.

With the formation of the different leagues of states and the declining significance of the feudal families in charge of the various states, these more formal exchanges constituted an ever smaller proportion of the diplomatic activity. By 493 B. C., Legge, paraphrasing one of the commentaries on the Tso-chuan observes "according to 'the rules of propriety,' the interchange of court visits between the princes should have been much more frequent. 'The rules of propriety' gave place to 'the way of the world.' Great States gave up those visits altogether, and small ones observed them by constraint not willingly."[20] The meetings of the various members of the leagues, and the diplomacy called for by the leagues constituted the main reason why diplomatic activity not only continued at a high rate but actually increased. Even the earliest alliance of the Chou states under the leadership of Duke Huan of Ch'i called for a great amount of diplomatic activity. A modern Chinese student of the Ch'un-ch'iu period, Li Tung-fang 黎東方 , lists 24 meetings, bilateral and multilateral, called by the Ch'i ruler between 681 and 644 B. C.[21]

A certain amount of the diplomatic activity of the Ch'un-ch'iu times was also carried on for economic reasons. The chronicles report many missions for the purpose of buying agricultural goods such as in 666 B. C., when a Lu minister went to Ch'i to buy grain to make up for a deficiency in Lu's crop of the former year.[22] State missions were also sent to arrange for trade agreements.[23] The greater part of the commerce between the states, however, was carried on by the merchants who were free to travel from state to state without many encumbrances.

By far the greatest part of the diplomatic activity of Ch'un-ch'iu times was occasioned by the quest for security or attempts to increase power on the part of the various states. This was especially true during the latter half of

the period. Princes or ministers of the states met to plan
military expeditions or to discuss mutual problems which
might someday call for military action. The rulers of Lu
and Ch'i met in 664 B. C., to plan an attack against the
Jung 戎 barbarians; ministers of Lu and Chin met in 616
B. C., to discuss the possible repercussions of several
of the smaller states formerly loyal to Chin having gone
over to the side of Ch'u.[24] Representatives met with
great frequency to plan mutual defense, to strengthen
ties of friendship, or to keep each other posted on their
activities. It was a general rule that a state should notify
its allies of any military expeditions which it contemplated,
whether it needed their help or not; and the state also
sent a mission to announce the result of the expedition.
Thus, for example, in 565 B. C. a Chin officer came to
Lu to announce to the duke of Lu, Chin's intention to
make an invasion of Cheng which was leaning toward the
side of Ch'u.[25]

One of the most interesting diplomatic episodes
recorded in the Ch'un-ch'iu and Tso-chuan was carried
on to bring the growing state of Wu into alliance with the
Chou states under Chin's leadership. Relations started
in 584 B. C., when Chin sent a military mission to Wu to
instruct the Wu armies in the latest methods of warfare
which Chin had developed.[26] Shortly after this, at the
initiative of Chin, representatives from Lu and some of
the smaller states started cultivating relations with Wu,
and finally Chin itself arranged a full-fledged military
alliance with Wu against Ch'u. Interestingly enough
although in the traditional Chou-centered view Wu was
one of the rude barbarian tribes and not worthy of dealing
with the Chou states on a footing of equality, when it
came to matters of security there was no hesitation about
entering into an alliance with it. There is nothing in either
the Ch'un-ch'iu or Tso-chuan to indicate that the negotia-
tions leading to the alliance in question were in any way
different from those carried on among the Chou states.

The legal reasons for the diplomatic activity which
was carried on by the Ch'un-ch'iu states were for the
most part derived from custom. Thus it could be considered almost a legal requirement that the states send
envoys to each other to acknowledge more formal missions.
Failure to do so was considered a serious breach of propriety. Likewise treaties signed with the leaders of the

leagues required a fixed number of missions to their
courts over a fixed period of time, and failure to send
these missions was the frequent occasion for punitive
expeditions. It was a fairly well-fixed rule after the time
of Duke Huan of Ch'i that the member states of the leagues
must send a minimum of one mission every three years
to the court of the league president, usually Chin, and
that the rulers themselves pay a court visit at least every
five years.[27]

The pattern which these diplomatic missions frequently followed was the exchange of missions between
two states followed usually by a treaty. A good illustration is recorded in the Ch'un-ch'iu starting in 566 B.C.
That year a Lu officer went to Wei on a mission of friendly
inquiries and to talk over mutual problems. This was
followed the same year by a mission of a Wei officer to
Lu both to acknowledge the Lu mission and to continue the
discussions. This resulted in a treaty which was in effect
a renewal of a treaty of 588 B.C. between Lu and Wei.[28]
Such treaties were also an important part of the interstate
life of Ch'un-ch'iu times, and it is important that we discuss them in some detail; but let us first point out one
other form of diplomatic activity which is frequently recorded in the early texts.

We refer to the sending of diplomatic notes or reports
in writing from one court to another. Frequently a well
composed note from a high official was more effective
in achieving the desired result than the dispatch of a
minor official. Therefore, the chief ministers of the
states would use the minor officials to carry their own
personal proposals and messages.[29] We have already
noted the success with which Tzu-ch'an utilized this form
of diplomacy, and his exchanges of letters with Shu
Hsiang. Almost three-quarters of a century earlier in
610 B.C., another Cheng minister, Tzu-chia子家 , utilized
this form to communicate with Chin. He carefully reviewed past relations between Chin and Cheng in order to
convince Chin of his state's complete loyalty, thus fore-
stalling a Chin invasion.[30] Such messages were also used
for propaganda purposes. In 578 B.C., for example, the
ruler of Chin sent a message to the court of Ch'in which
in effect broke off relations between the two states--war
usually followed quickly after such a formal breakoff--
but he also utilized the opportunity to review in great

detail the relations between Chin and Ch'in over a long
period of time. This "white paper" was certainly not a
fair representation of the past, yet facts and dates were
cited in such a way as to make Ch'in appear the obvious
villain. Presumably it was intended for the consumption
of the representatives of the other states who were at the
Ch'in court when Chin's messenger read it aloud to the
chief minister of Ch'in.[31]

The most formal documents involved in the relations
between the states of the Ch'un-ch'iu period were the
treaties.[32] These are designated in the chronicles by the
word meng 盟 which is perhaps more literally translated
covenant. The term usually refers to the whole of the
ceremony by which states joined in a pact, rather than
to the pact itself. After long discussions about the terms
of the treaties to be signed, the representatives partici-
pated in a very solemn ritual in which an animal--usually
a calf--was sacrificed at some holy spot outside the walls
of a city. The left ear of the sacrificial victim was cut
off and it was used to smear with blood both the document
bearing the articles of agreement, and the lips of the
principals. One copy of the document was buried with the
sacrificial beast and each of the signatories kept a copy.[33]

The texts of these treaties were couched in brief but
solemn language and usually involved three parts: the
statement of purpose, the articles of agreement, and an
oath invoking the wrath of the most important deities
upon anyone who transgressed the agreements. Most of
the treaties expressed many lofty aspirations and high
ideals; and had but a small fraction of those recorded
been carried out, there would be little interstate conflict
to record here. In all, more than 140 treaties are recorded
in the Ch'un-ch'iu. Of these 72 were bilateral.[34]

Bilateral treaties were concluded for many purposes:
mutual defense, trade, marriage alliance, and for the
sake of traditional friendship.[35] The bilateral pacts pre-
dominate in the early years of the Ch'un-ch'iu, but with
the hegemony of Duke Huan of Ch'i the states came to
rely more upon the meetings of the leagues to settle their
problems; and the greater number of the recorded treaties
became multilateral. It was only with the decline of Chin
power toward the close of the sixth century B.C. that a
system of bilateral alliances again became predominant.
Perhaps an extreme example of the bilateral type of treaty

was the abortive attempt in 579 B.C. to bring about peace
between the traditional rivals Chin and Ch'u. As in the
general disarmament attempt thirty-five years later,
which we have discussed above, a statesman from Sung
was the instigator; this time it was a minister by name
of <u>Hua Yüan</u> 華元. He managed to persuade the rulers of
Chin and Ch'u to sign a treaty of friendship and mutual
aid the provisions of which read:

1. Ch'u and Chin shall not go to war with each
   other.
2. They shall have common likings and dislikings.
3. They shall compassionate States that are in
   calamity and peril, and be ready to relieve
   such as are unfortunate.
4. Chin shall attack any that would injure Ch'u,
   and Ch'u any that would injure Chin.
5. Their roads shall be open to messengers
   that wish to pass with offerings from the
   one to the other.
6. They shall take measures against the disaffected, and punish those who do not appear
   in the royal court.

Whoever shall violate this covenant, may the intelligent spirits destroy him, causing defeat to his
armies, and a speedy end to his possession of his
state.[36]

This treaty was concluded with all the formal and religious
ceremonies, and by its wording we would expect that there
should be no further enmity to record between Chin and
Ch'u.

But this was flying in the face of reality: Chin and
Ch'u as leaders of powerful leagues of states were bound
to be rivals. Why then did they even bother with this
scrap of paper? We know the reason in Chin's case, and
we also know that it was not taken too seriously by Ch'u.
Chin was willing to conclude the pact in hopes of securing
its left flank against Ch'u for an attack which it planned
and carried out against Ch'in the next year, 578 B.C.[37]
That Ch'u regarded the pact as hardly more than a temporary measure can be seen in the fact that three years

later, in 576 B. C. it dispatched a military force to the
north against Chin. Before the decision to attack was
made, at least one Ch'u official wondered, "Is it not
improper to violate the covenant which we made so recently with Chin?" It was at this time that the Ch'u general
Tzu-fan made the statement which we have quoted above:
"When we can gain an advantage over our enemies, we
must advance, without any consideration of covenants."
Note that despite the idealistic phrasing of the treaty,
Chin was still identified as the enemy state.[38]

Not all the bilateral pacts, however, were treated
so lightly. When they were concluded between states
whose positions made them, so to speak, natural allies,
the provisions were carried out with great rigor; and the
treaties were renewed many times. The Lu chronicle
reports, for example, in 588 B. C., that the Duke of Lu
renewed two covenants that year, one with Chin which had
been concluded in 590 B. C., and one with Wei which had
been signed in 602 B. C. It is interesting to note that on
this occasion Chin sent a minister of 3rd degree while
Wei sent one of 1st degree in rank. There was some
question as to which of the two treaties of renewal should
be signed first. The Lu officers advised giving precedence
to the minister from the stronger state, regardless of
rank.[39]

Most of the multilateral treaties recorded in the
Ch'un-ch'iu period were signed in connection with a
meeting of one of the leagues of states. They usually
carried more weight with the individual states because
there were provisions for joint action on the part of the
other signatories against any state which violated the
provisions. Thus, for example, Chin, Sung, Wei, and
Ts'ao signed a treaty in 579 B. C., to the effect that "they
would compassionate states which were in distress and
punish those which were disaffected."[40] The covenant
signed by the Chou league under the direction of Duke
Wen of Chin in 632 B. C., read:

We will all assist the royal house, and do no
harm to one another.

If any one transgresses this covenant, may the
intelligent Spirits destroy him, so that he shall
lose his people and not be able to possess his

State, and, to the remotest posterity, let him
have no descendant old or young. [41]

That mutual enforcement was understood can be seen in
the fact that all the signatories except Cheng met the next
year to plan an attack against Cheng, whom they felt to be
violating the pact by leaning toward Ch'u. [42]

The covenant of mutual aid which was signed in 562
B. C., by twelve of the Chou states included perhaps as
many states of the Chou league as any treaty recorded in
the Ch'un-ch'iu; and its wording was accordingly impres-
sive:

All we who covenant together agree

1. Not to hoard up the produce of good years
2. Not to shut one another out from advantages
3. Not to protect traitors
4. Not to shelter criminals
5. To aid one another in disasters and calamities
6. To have compassion on one another in seasons
   of misfortune and disorder
7. To cherish the same likings and dislikings
8. To support and encourage the royal House.

Should any prince break these engagements, may
He who watches over men's sincerity and He who
watches over covenants, (the spirits of) the
famous hills and the famous streams, the kings
and dukes of our predecessors, the whole host
of Spirits, and all who are sacrificed to, the
ancestors of our 12 States with their 7 surnames:
--may all these intelligent Spirits destroy him,
so that he shall lose his people, his appointment
pass from him, his family perish, and his State
be utterly overthrown. [43]

In times when religious superstitions still weighed heavily
in the conduct of affairs, the oath recorded in this treaty
was indeed a formidable one. Yet the very next year there
is a record of hostilities between two of the states which
signed the pact, Chü 莒 and Lu. [44]

If even the most solemn of agreements were violated
in so short a time, what then were the guarantees which

the states relied on to keep the treaties in force, and why were they not more effective? In addition to the provisions for mutual enforcement which we have noted in the multi-partite treaties, and the solemn oaths whose importance should not be underestimated, there were other systems of guarantees in use. [45] In some cases the states posted a bond for their conformance to treaty provisions. In 571 B. C., for example, the Chou states held the city of Hu-lao 虎牢, which belonged to Cheng, as a bond for Cheng's good faith in carrying out treaty provisions. [46] A more common practice was the exchange of hostages, chih 質. This was the method for guaranteeing the enforcement of a great number of the bilateral treaties. Important persons from each state were sent to the other state, to be put to death if faith were broken. Most commonly these hostages were the sons of the rulers. In 643 B. C., the eldest son of the ruler of Chin was sent to Ch'in as a hostage. Another example occurred in 610 B. C., when Chin and Cheng exchanged hostages. [47]

Another type of hostage, of course, was the daughter or son from an outside state who was married to a child of the ruler. These marriage alliances were frequently used to buttress treaty arrangements. There was a danger, however, that the outside state might support the claims to the throne of any offspring of such a marriage and thus succeed in setting up a satellite or puppet government. The rulers of the Ch'un-ch'iu period appreciated the value of supporting claimants to power in other states on even the most tenuous grounds; and, indeed, the use of satellite parties and puppet regimes was one of the most important strategies for state expansion. The contemporary scholar Chao Ch'ih-tzu has pointed out thirty-six cases in Ch'un-ch'iu times in which the expanding power relied upon such fifth columns within the territory of its victim. In some cases indirect support to the claimant was sufficient, but more often a fostered civil war was combined with invasion. [48]

There was another factor which worked in favor of the enforcement of treaties, and that was the desirability of having a reputation for good faith. Such a reputation was important in attracting allies or in gaining the support of one of the great powers in a treaty of mutual assistance. The great powers themselves were especially anxious for a reputation of good faith, for it could sometimes be the basis on which the in-between states chose between them and their rivals. Thus, although this factor of interstate morality did rest upon the principle of self-interest, it nevertheless frequently worked for the maintenance of good faith in interstate relations.[49] We have noted the important part it played in the solid backing which the Chou states gave to Duke Wen of Chin.

In general, the leagues of states were the most effective means of enforcement, not only of the treaties but also of the rules of interstate law in Ch'un-ch'iu times. These leagues or alliances of states came to play an increasingly important role in interstate life from the formation of the first Chou league in 680 B. C., until near the end of the Ch'un-ch'iu period. The sources which have been preserved limit our knowledge of these leagues mainly to two groups, the Chou states and the states which united under the banner of Ch'u. But there are indications that Ch'in was a consistent center of power and leader of a league of states in the West and that in the latter half of the Ch'un-ch'iu, Wu headed a league of states in the southeast. Although when one league confronted another, wars were bound to become larger in scope, yet they occurred less frequently because for the sake of security and solidarity, the members of a league were obliged to maintain as much harmony within their area as possible. This meant that the members of a league had to conform as much as possible to the laws, either as agreed upon mutually, laid down by the leader, or handed down by custom.

The position of leader of a league involved both advantages and disadvantages to the state which filled it. Among the advantages were the facts that the smaller member states sent tribute to the court of the leader, the leader could effectively direct the general policies and alignments of league members, and the state of the leader was usually protected from the devastations of military incursions because it was surrounded with the buffer of satellites. Disadvantages included the fact that the league leader usually had to maintain a large fighting force and come to the aid of the league members on all sides.

These leagues of states served many functions besides the main one of collective security for which they were organized. One type of activity in which they aided was the peaceful settlement of disputes between their members.

The Ch'un-ch'iu reports many cases of mediation, arbitration and even intervention within both the Chou and
Ch'u leagues. These methods of settlement developed to
prevent disputes which might have weakened the power
of either league. In most cases the court of the league
leader served as the high tribunal. Occasionally, however,
in the Chin league most members of which gave ritual
allegiance to the Chou court, the Chou ruler rather than
the hegemon served as a tribunal for the settlement of
disputes. Most of the works on the interstate law of the
Ch'un-ch'iu which we have listed above discuss in great
detail the examples of pacific settlement of disputes. A
few cases should suffice for purposes of illustration.[50]

In 587 B. C., a dispute arose between Cheng, which
was at that time closely allied to Ch'u, and little Hsü 許,
over a tract of land at their borders. Ch'u sent its general
Tzu-fan 子反 to prevent any outbreak of hostilities; "and
the earl of Cheng and the baron of Hsü sued each other,
Huang Shu 皇戌 pleading the case for the earl. Tzu-fan
could not determine the matter in dispute, and said, 'If
you two princes will go before my ruler, then he and
some of his ministers will hear together what you want
to prove, and the merits of your case can be known.' "[51]
The following year the rulers of Cheng and Hsü appeared
at the Ch'u court and the case was settled there in Hsü's
favor. Cheng, unhappy with the decision, started once
again to lean in favor of the Chou league.[52] Again, a dispute about who was to blame for an armed clash which
had occurred between men of Chu and Lu was settled at
the Chin court in 519 B. C.[53]

In case of a dispute between the league leader and
one of the member states, usually a third member of the
league offered to mediate the dispute. In 625 B. C., Wei
and Chin were having a serious dispute which threatened
to lead to war. Wei was in a position from which it could
not retreat with any dignity, and yet a war against the
powerful armies of Chin would have been disastrous.
Accordingly, Wei requested Ch'en 陳 to mediate the dispute, which it did, successfully.[54] The following year,
624 B. C., the Ch'un-ch'iu records that the Wei ruler
himself went to Ch'en to thank that state for its mediation.[5]
An example of mediation by the Chou court occurred in
636 B. C., when the Chou king was mediator in a dispute
between Cheng and the little state of Hua 滑.[56]

Occasionally the league leader would call for forceful intervention by one of the member states to settle a dispute which seemed to threaten the security of the league. It was considered a grave breach of interstate and league rules for one of the states to assume such a responsibility without first having the permission of the league leader. In fact, any military action inside a league without prior assent of the president of covenants, <u>meng-chu</u> 盟主, was a serious offense. In 605 B. C., Lu and Ch'i intervened with force to settle a dispute between Chü 莒 and T'an 郯 which had been disturbing the peace in the East. At this time, Chin was actively engaged against Ch'in, and Ch'i had taken upon itself active leadership of the eastern states for a few years. The later critics nevertheless condemn the action as contrary to the rules.[57] Lu was usually very circumspect in its observance of all the rules. In 569 B. C., it obtained permission from Chin to undertake a military action against Tseng 鄫, and again in 544 B. C., a Lu diplomat received the hegemon's permission to continue its expansion against the eastern state of Chi 杞.[58] Before the decision on the latter application of Lu for permission to undertake military operations there was some discussion at the Chin court as to whether Lu was not too ambitious and was not becoming too strong. A Chin officer, friendly to Lu, carried the day with the following argument, which illustrates some of the points which we have made with reference to relations between league leaders and members:

Chi is a remnant of (the House of) Hsia, and has assimilated to the wild tribes to the east. (The princes of) Lu are the descendants of the duke of Chou, and are in most friendly relations with Chin; if we should confer all Chi on Lu, we should not be doing anything strange, so that there is nothing to make to do about (in the present matter). In its relations with Chin, Lu contributes its dues without fail; its valuable curiosities are always arriving; its princes, ministers and great officers come, one after another, to our court. Our historiographers do not cease recording; our treasury is not left empty a month. Let such a state of things alone. Why should we make Lu thin in order to fatten Chi?[59]

One of the fields of interstate law in which the rules
did undergo some change during the Ch'un-ch'iu period
as a result of the growing importance of the leagues was
that concerned with the right of asylum. In his study of
the first twenty years of the Ch'un-ch'iu Roswell Britton
points out that there was "a general acknowledgment of
a right of asylum among the nobility of the nothern states."[6]
This rule continued to carry some weight, but opposed to
it were the growing number of treaty clauses providing
for extradition of criminals and traitors, as, for example,
clauses three and four in the multilateral treaty quoted
above. It became ever more difficult for the political
refugee to find a safe place of refuge; from the point of
view of his state he was both a traitor and a criminal. If
he wished to find a haven, it would have to be outside the
confines of league territory. Thus through the Spring and
Autumn period we find more and more examples of political
refugees being captured by league members for other
league members. This is especially true of refugees
from Chin, most of the time leader of the league of Chou
states. Many commentators treat the right of asylum as
something which remained rather constant throughout the
period, and merely comment upon those occasions where
it did not hold. The extent to which the rule of extradition
of political criminals had replaced the right of asylum is
indicated by the fact that Chin returned the viscount of the
Man-Jung 蠻戎 to its rival Ch'u in 491 B. C. In doing so,
the Chin ruler made allusions to the Covenant of 546 B. C.,
most of the provisions of which had long since been violated
Dr. Legge observes here, "The act of Chin in this matter
is held to have been disgraceful to it. The right of asylum
for refugees seems to have been accorded by the States to
one another; and one which had played such a part as Chin
ought to have maintained it with peculiar jealousy."[61]

Another indirect service which the leagues undoubtedly
performed was to stimulate trade, communications, and
cultural interchange. From the first meeting of the states
under Duke Huan of Ch'i in 681 B. C., the members of the
Chou league of states averaged two meetings in every
three years until the end of the Ch'un-ch'iu. These meetings were not small affairs. A delegation with its retainers
often numbered over one hundred members; and merchants
from the same state frequently went along to the meeting
to trade with members of the other delegations. This meant

that most of the meetings of the states had to be held in
the larger cities, and these cities profited greatly from
the extended stay of so many visitors. The frequent passage of these large delegations also served to stimulate
road building and to improve the means of communication,
since each delegation attempted to keep in close touch
with its home territory.[62]

A word must be added about the place of Chou itself
in the league which paid at least lip service to its superior
place. After the first few meetings of the League under
Ch'i's leadership, it became customary for the Chou king
to send a representative to be present at the meetings.
The various presidents of the league welcomed these
representatives, for they gave an air of legitimacy to the
leaders' claims to superiority. The support of the Chou
ruler encouraged the smaller states to cooperate since
they felt that his participation insured their continued
existence. The Ch'un-ch'iu, however, leaves us in no
doubt that Chou was just another weak member. It even
records instances in which the Chou representative signed
covenants resulting from conferences on a footing of
equality with the other states.[63] Whenever possible the
league president utilized the symbol of allegiance to Chou
as a buttress for his own position; but if circumstances
demanded, there was no hesitation about ignoring the
wishes of the Chou king. Thus, in the Chou area at least,
the league organization aided to a limited extent in state
preservation.

In the southern league under Ch'u's leadership, this
air of legitimacy was very obviously lacking. This perhaps
accounts for the fact that Ch'u had to place more reliance
upon military force to hold its allies and was more frequently obliged to extinguish the states in its area. There
was no moral restraint placed upon its treatment of its
allies, and this was probably Ch'u's chief element of
weakness. Ch'u did borrow upon Chou's prestige for a
short time following the conference of 546 B. C., when,
as we have indicated above, members of the Chou league
under Chin and Ch'u's member states paid visits to the
courts of both league presidents. Even though this arrangement lasted but a few years, it must have had an important
part in increasing contacts between league areas.[64]

The various leagues of states, then, did play an
important role not only in creating and enforcing rules

of interstate intercourse but also in providing a certain
uniformity in state behavior patterns. These patterns
were, however, little more than patterns of convenience
in a power struggle; and it now behooves us to examine
some of the cases where they did not hold up, and to offer
some sort of an answer to the question "Why?" These
cases where the interstate law did not hold up were after
all the important cases. In view of the weight attached
to the slightest ceremonial details, it would hardly be
expected that the law would be violated in matters which
were not important.

In general, the rules which governed the intercourse
among the states of the Ch'un-ch'iu period prevailed only
where they were mutually beneficial. In the very first
years, when most of the rulers of the states were still
relatively insecure in their positions, the right of asylum
was uniformly granted because few rulers were sure that
they might not someday be political refugees themselves.[65]
Again, it was similarly mutually beneficial to grant diplomatic immunity. Throughout the period, there was the
overall expectation that the state which adhered closely
to the rules had a better than even chance against another
state of comparatively equal power which violated them.
A few years after the conference of 546 B.C., a statesman of Cheng expressed to Shu Hsiang, the leader of a
Chin embassy which was passing through Cheng on its
way to the Ch'u court, apprehension about the plans of
Ch'u. "The extravagance of the king of Ch'u is excessive;
you must be on your guard against it," he warned. Shu
Hsiang's reply probably fairly represents the attitude of
those who placed faith in adherence to the law as a main
prop of security:

> His excessive extravagance, replied Shu Hsiang,
> will be calamitous to himself, but how can it
> affect others? If we present our offerings, and
> be careful of our deportment, maintaining our
> good faith, and observing the rules of propriety,
> reverently attentive to our first proceedings
> and thinking at the same time of our last, so
> that all might be done over again; if we comply
> [with his requirements] so as not to lose our
> decorum, and, while respectful, do not lose
> our dignity; if our communications be according

> to the lessons (of wisdom), our service be per-
> formed according to the laws of antiquity, and
> our duty be discharged according to [the rules
> of] the ancient kings, and regulated by a con-
> sideration of [what is due to] our two States,
> however extravagant he be, what can he do to
> us?[66]

Such a statement of expectations was easy for a Chin
representative to make. Chin was not only a match for
Ch'u in power, but if it were thus attentive to the rules,
it could count on the moral support of Chou. If, on the
other hand, Chin itself showed ambitious designs in its
relations with Ch'u, it might cause some of the smaller
states on its fringes to transfer their loyalty to Ch'u. In
its dealings with the smaller states well within its own
orbit, however, Chin did not have to be so careful; and,
indeed, it was not. For example, in 580 B.C., Chin
detained the ruler of Lu at its court and kept him a virtual
prisoner. Again in 519 B.C., it seized the Lu ambassador
Shu-sun She 叔孫舍 and held him prisoner for a while.[67]
In both these cases it violated the accepted rule of diplomatic immunity; but it had little to fear from the state of
Lu, and the results achieved outweighed any possible
distrust aroused among other members of the league each
time. In general, the great powers could and did act with
less consideration of rules. Adherence to the law in any
instance usually involved a power calculation by the state
in question. If the penalties for non-adherence outweighed
the advantages to be gained by non-adherence, then the
law was obeyed. This was usually the case mainly for the
lesser powers.

In their struggles with each other, the big powers
seldom found it more advantageous to hold to the rule.
For example, they frequently violated the rule that a
state should not be invaded in the year in which a ruler
had died or in which there had been an insurrection within
the state. In 560 B.C., Wu invaded Ch'u whose ruler had
died; and again in 515 B.C., it took advantage of the con-
fusion caused by the death of a Ch'u king to invade that
land.[68] In 571 B.C., Chin led a force into Cheng the ruler
of which, Duke Ch'eng 成公, had just died. This was at
a time when Chin needed every possible advantage in its
struggle with Ch'u. Since Chin was acting for the Chou

states, the traditional commentaries have little to say on this breach of interstate law.[69] In 676 B. C., Pa 巴 took advantage of an insurrection in Ch'u to invade it. At that time Pa was the great rival of Ch'u in the southwest.[70]

An excellent example of a case where rules and treaties had little weight in the struggles between the powers occurred in 627 B. C. At that time a Chin minister noticed that there was a great amount of dissatisfaction among the people of Ch'in. "...this is an opportunity given us by Heaven. It should not be lost," he said. The Chin ruler objected to this statement, pointing out that Ch'in had helped to put the former Chin ruler Duke Wen on the throne and was by treaty a friendly power. Yet the minister insisted that Ch'in was the natural enemy. "Ch'in has shown no sympathy with us in our loss (the death of Ch'ung-erh)...It is Ch'in who has been unobservant of propriety; what have we to do with former favors? I have heard that if you let your enemy go a single day, you are preparing the misfortunes of several generations." Accordingly Chin did attack Ch'in and won the engagement.[71]

Still another violation of rules by Chin is recorded by Tso in 582 B. C. "In autumn, the earl of Cheng went to Chin, the people of which, to punish him for his disaffection, and inclining to Ch'u, seized him in T'ung-ti 銅鞮. Luan-shu 欒書 then invaded Cheng which sent Po-chüan 伯蠲 to go and obtain peace. The people of Chin, however, put him to death, which was contrary to the rule;--during hostilities messengers may go and come between the parties."[72]

These few examples of cases where expectations of state behavior, based upon interstate law, broke down should be sufficient to point out what was actually the only important uniformity in state behavior in the Ch'un-ch'iu period; that is, a central regard for state power. With respect to the law, even adherence to the most minor rules of interstate intercourse depended upon a power calculation. In diplomacy, we have seen that the former system (if it actually did exist) of ranking states by the title of their rulers gave place to a system of precedence by power.[73] Again, we have noted that the supposedly superior Chou states did not hesitate in their struggle with Ch'u,[74] to deal with Wu on a footing of equality.

Even in those cases where the legal methods of settlement seemed to work, the power considerations of the
states weighed most heavily. In 614 B. C., when Lu medi-
ated successfully for Wei and Cheng at Chin, it is not
sufficient, as the students of Ch'un-ch'iu interstate law
mentioned above have done, merely to note that this was
a case where mediation worked. It is necessary to note
also that at that time Chin was probably only too happy
to have its difficulties with Wei and Cheng settled, since
it was being forced to guard its borders against Ch'in.[75]

Thus in the Spring and Autumn times, under such a
system, the greatest hope for peace and the establishment of interstate intercourse based upon law would
seem to have been to expand the area of mutual benefit
where the advantages of obedience to the law consistently
outweighed those of breaking the law. This was generally
the case within the leagues; and for the short time after
546 B. C., the area expanded to include both the Chin and
Ch'u controlled states--an unplanned result of a disarmament conference. But in a time when several large
sovereign states were struggling for superiority, such
a hope remained unrealized. Some of the great men of
the Ch'un-ch'iu, such as Tzu-ch'an, recognized the situation for what it was and tried to ameliorate it in their
own time.

Another group of individuals, the philosophers,
sought for an overall answer to the problem of conflict
which continued on through the Chan-kuo times. Some
of these philosophers sought the answer in institutions;
Confucius through an idealization of former Chou unity;
the legalists through a rigid system of laws. Others
turned to an examination of man's basic nature: those
who followed Confucius, and especially Mencius, declared that man's nature was fundamentally good and
could be turned from conflict under the ideal Chou system
of exemplary rule; those who followed the legalist argument, influenced by Hsün-tzu, declared it to be fundamentally evil and that stringent measures and harsh control were required to prevent conflict. It took a combination of both approaches to bring the peace and unity which
came under the Han dynasty, in the second century before
the Christian era.

Chapter VII

A RECONSIDERATION OF THE CH'UN-CH'IU PERIOD

This analysis of the sovereign state system of the Spring and Autumn period in Chinese history has of necessity omitted many names and events which belong in a standard history. Yet such an approach does offer further data for an understanding of the period--data which most of the narrative histories (especially those in the West) have failed to present. The findings of our political analysis have in general confirmed the interpretation of Ch'un-ch'iu history advanced by Ku Chieh-kang and his associates; and, thus, to those who have followed the stimulating course of modern Chinese historiography, they are not essentially new. It is valuable, nevertheless, to pull together some general conclusions on this period which derive from our analysis and the new historiography.

Let us start by pointing out again that if we look for an account of political development and great institutional change rather than moralistic editing, the Ch'un-ch'iu chronicle is an admirable and consistent document. It records a pattern of state development from 722 to 481 B. C. which is regular and quite understandable. Confucius, who preferred to be known as a transmitter, surely had great historical wisdom. A vital tale and a political lesson are adequately given in the bald chronicle which he edited. He lived in an age when the sovereign state was establishing itself as the highest moral end and in which the relationships among these sovereign units were therefore less and less subject to any moral code. The individual human was no longer the center of concern.

We know, of course, of the developments in China in the centuries following the death of Confucius. These developments were a consistent projection of the trends which the sage of Lu had faithfully transmitted in the Annals of his state. Small wonder, then, that he felt this to be the work by which men would come to know him, or condemn him.

The Ch'un-ch'iu records an era of political innova-
tion and consolidation, not a period of disintegration as the
traditional scholars would have us believe. There probably never was much of a Chou empire to disintegrate,
and such a term is hardly apt for describing the gradual
disappearance of feudalism. The Ch'un-ch'iu period
brought increasing contact and cultural interchange
among many independent areas.[1] During this time the
conditions were created which were to make possible the
first unification of all China under one rule some centuries
later.

The most striking development during this period
was the expansion and consolidation of state power, both
internal and external. As in the study of the growth of
state power in the West, the outward growth has called for
most comment, and the inward growth has not been very
much noticed. Bertrande de Jouvenel lists three
"ponderables" for charting the advance of internal power:
the dimensions of armies, the weight of taxation, and the
number of officials.[2] Surely, on all of these scores the
Ch'un-ch'iu period is a most important age in the history
of political power in China. Political power became more
and more something impersonal in the hands of a bureaucratic apparatus whose major goal was to serve the
impersonal ideal of the state.

The inner growth of state power is also observable
in the increased number of service functions performed
by the state. During the Spring and Autumn Period the
state was reaching its tentacles ever more deeply into the
lives of the people. Large-scale irrigation and construction measures, grain collection and storage by the state,
the construction of walled cities and other such activities
required impersonal regulations and decrees by the
central authority. These activities and the various other
state monopolies stemming from the time of Kuan-tzu
were also "ponderables" in the growth of state power.[3]

Such developments called for order and discipline,
and so it was to be expected that the "great political
tendency of the time was a movement . . . toward a
government by rulers possessing absolute power, from a
government by customary morality (li), and by individuals,
to government by law."[4] Certainly this disappearance of
the human factor with the growth of state power was one

of the trends which made Confucius apprehensive. We can safely say that most of the important elements of feudalism had thus disappeared by the closing years of the Ch'un-ch'iu period. Ch'i Ssu-ho prefers to believe that Chou feudalism lasted throughout the Ch'un-ch'iu and that its various aspects began to disappear in Chan-kuo times.[5] But the Chan-kuo period was merely a carrying out on a larger scale of the great changes which had already taken place before.

The growth of internal state power was, of course, in reciprocal relation with the economic and social changes which were taking place at the same time. Although these have been only of indirect concern here, it must be remarked that much of the recent Chinese and Japanese scholarship in these fields deserves to be pulled together in the interest of a more accurate history of the period.

Our major concern has been with the external expansion of state power during the Ch'un-ch'iu and the developing relationships involved. Expansion, we have noted, was at the expense of the weak. At first small feudal cities expanded to absorb surrounding territory or buffer area. Then when they came into contact and conflict with each other, the stronger cities began to take over the weaker and constitute themselves states. The more powerful states then continued the expansion process by absorbing the weaker ones which had become the new buffer areas. Relations between the larger states picked up at a rapid pace, aiding in turn the development of interstate commerce, the development of better means of communication, and the exchange of ideas. State expanison meant a constant decrease in the number of states, and this trend continued until it produced the eventual unification of China.

It is interesting to observe that the methods developed by the great powers Chin and Ch'u for absorbing the weaker states provided a basis for the later unification. The more totalitarian Ch'in dynasty followed the pattern set by Ch'u in the Ch'un-ch'iu. It allowed practically no autonomy to the states which it conquered. The Han dynasty reverted to the less rigid method of granting more local autonomy, which had been successfully utilized by Chin.

Agreement on the multi-state character of politics in Ancient China eliminates many of the contradictions which

have plagued those who have attempted to maintain the
fiction of Chou unity. Thus, there is no need to explain
why some states had five main officers and others six,
why some armies were organized differently than others,
etc. These contradictions have for centuries troubled
traditional Chinese scholars whose understandable tendency to treat China as a whole has prevented them from
finding the obvious answer.

With regard to the operation of the multi-state
system we have seen that the ultimate aim of political
actions was the expression of the sovereignty of the
individual states. This became the standard for judging
the measures of the rulers and the various officers of the
states. The moral code of the former Chou feudal age
had meaning only when it added to the power and prestige
of the state which claimed to adhere to it. The ritual
framework of the feudal tradition could at times serve as
a code of conduct for the individual states, but this code
carried little weight unless power considerations argued
in favor of adherence.

The trend was toward the development of leagues or
blocs of states, and these groupings fostered a semblance
of order and peace within the confines of their areas of
influence. Here rules of interstate conduct prevailed
because they worked in favor of the solidarity of the
alliance. Religious or cultural ties, while important, were
never the decisive factor in the foreign policies of the
states. If necessity demanded they would not hesitate to
form alliances with even the most uncultured barbarians
outside their area. Chin's turning to an alliance with Wu
is probably the most dramatic example which we have
noted.

Throughout the period the policies, both internal and
external, of the states had to be formulated on the basis
of the expectation of violence. In the absence of a higher
authority war was the final arbiter. The appeals of the
philosophers and prophets to establish their moral codes
as the highest authority fell on deaf ears, for there was
never any guarantee that acceptance would be universal.
Thus the major concern of the rulers and their ministers
was the quest for state power and the maintenance of a
constant state of military preparedness and alertness.
This situation did much to aid in the internal expansion
of state power, for only thorough organization and control

could give the military preparedness which the times
demanded. The lessons of the past were apparent to the
leaders of all the states which survived. The _Annals_
demonstrate that those states which were neither strong
nor prepared had little hope of survival under a system
in which force decided issues. The Chou states preserved
their customs and culture by organizing a strong military
alliance among themselves and by alliances with outer
powers whenever necessary.

Thus, major policies were security policies. Security
and power were the concern of the day. Such actions as
rounding out frontiers, joining leagues, transferring
alliances, treaty arrangements, fomenting civil war else-
where can all be interpreted in terms of the quest for
security. Each of the great powers suspected the other
great powers of ambition to rule all of their world, and
this was prevented during Ch'un-ch'iu times only by a
strategy of balance of power which accounts for the many
diplomatic revolutions recorded.

Such a balancing process placed a premium on the
ability to determine which was the major threat power.
During Ch'un-ch'iu times the statesmen were successful
in preventing the upset of the balance, but it was at the
cost of the extinction of many smaller states and much
bloodshed. The most consistently threatening power was
Ch'u. Later in Chan-kuo times the statesmen failed to
appreciate the collapse of Ch'u's power potential and
likewise failed to take into account the quiet growth of
Ch'in under a totalitarian rule in the West. By the time
Ch'in was ready for its grand bid for control, the patriotism and insistence on sovereign rights of the other six
major powers to its east prevented them from uniting to
meet the threat. They did form an Alliance of Six Kingdoms in 333 B.C. for the purpose of resisting Ch'in, but
it lasted only briefly. One by one Ch'in conquered the
other states and imposed on them a new type of political
control, destroying their cultures and records. The Ch'in
organization, for the most part the creation of Lord Shang
(in power from 361 to 338 B.C.) was the climax of the
development of state power which we noted in Ch'un-ch'iu
times. It involved division of the land in a new system
which gave the state more direct control, new forms of
state taxes, and a method of controlling people by mutual
responsibility and fear.[6]

Certainly the ultimate victory of Ch'in could have been predicted on the basis of Ch'un-ch'iu experience, and indeed some of the statesmen of the Chan-kuo made the right prediction. The history of the Spring and Autumn Period shows clearly that the states with the most internal unity and control were victorious in war. The constant tension placed a premium on morale through discipline and internal order.

Another observation must be made about the multi-state system of ancient China. Within such a system neutrality was an impossible and futile hope. Those states which attempted to remain neutral usually suffered extinction at the hands of one of the power blocs which saw them as the answer to swinging the balance in its favor. For this reason many of the states gave allegiance to the Chou league which allowed them some cultural and political autonomy rather than suffer the fate of former "neutrals" which had fallen to Ch'u.

The closest approach to peace in Ch'un-ch'iu China came with a relatively stable balance of power between the two great alliances of the mid-sixth century B. C. under the leadership of Chin and Ch'u. But even the statesmen of the time realized that the balance could not last, and they expressed their apprehension. They knew that wars between the great leagues had become increasingly devastating and lasted longer. By the closing years of the Ch'un-ch'iu period, the people found themselves in very much the same situation as that which faces the world today. Larger states had improved the methods of warfare, but no one had to any comparable degree improved the methods of avoiding war save enforced unity under a totalitarian regime.

NOTES

Chapter I

1. Carl J. Friedrich, Inevitable Peace, Cambridge, Mass., Harvard University Press, 1948.

2. W. T. R. Fox, "Interwar international relations research: the American experience," World Politics, Vol. 2, No. 1, October 1949, p. 69.

3. Ibid, p. 71, note 3.

4. For a realistic appraisal of the UNESCO aims and efforts see F. S. Dunn, War and the Minds of Men, New York, Harper, 1950.

5. F. S. Dunn, "The present course of international relations research," World Politics, Vol. 2, No. 1, October 1949, pp. 80-95.

6. For example, Coleman Phillipson, International Law and Custom of Ancient Greece and Rome, New York, 1911, 2 volumes.

7. Narendra Nath Law, Interstate Relations in Ancient India, London, Luzac and Co. , 1920.

Chapter II

1. See, for example, Chang Lung-yen 張龍炎 "History of Yin Dynasty as Reconstructed from the late Discoveries," 殷史蠡測 , Nanking Journal, Vol. I, No. 1, May 1931, pp. 151-188. Chang gives, on the basis of the recent excavations, a detailed discussion of many sides of Yin culture including society (clothing, food, housing, communications, etc.), economics, government, ritual customs, chronology, and living conditions. Recent works in English covering the Shang culture include two volumes by Professor H. G. Creel: The Birth of China, London, 1936 and Studies in Early Chinese Culture, First Series (ACLS Studies in Chinese and related civilizations) No. 3, Baltimore, 1937. Equally important in adding to our knowledge of the Shang period have been the studies made of the bones used then for divination purposes. A brief summary of some of the work which has been done in this field and some of the results obtained can be found in Chou Chuan-ju's article "The Study of Inscriptions on the Oracle Bones" translated by A. J. Schwarz in Philobiblon,

No. 1, June 1946, pp. 3-12. Preeminent in this field is the Chinese scholar Tung Tso-pin 董作賓 of National Taiwan University. His works together with the many important contributions of the Japanese scholars who have studied Shang culture are listed by E. Stuart Kirby, Introduction to the Economic History of China, Chapters V and VI. This brilliant forthcoming book appeared serially in the Far Eastern Economic Review, Hong Kong, 1952-1953. Professor Kirby has amassed in critical interpretive fashion a bibliographic account of the latest developments in Chinese historiography with particular focus on economic history. His appraisal of the work of Japanese scholars during World War II is especially valuable.

2. Lou Kan-jou, Histoire sociale de l'époque Tcheou, Paris, 1935, supports the previous opinions of Wang Kuo-wei and Kuo Mo-jo on the clan basis of Shang political control, pp. 107ff. Kirby, op. cit., Chapter VI.

3. There seems to be little dispute about Chou's introduction of formalized feudal institutions into China. See Lou Kan-jou, p. 113, and Kirby, Chapter VI. Professor K. A. Wittfogel has pointed out that many of the elements of the Chou feudalism were in existence in Shang times ("The Foundations and Stages of Chinese Economic History," Zeitschrift für Sozialforschung, IV, 1935, pp. 26-58), and recent works by Chinese and Japanese scholars bear out the conclusion that some of the Chou feudal practices found their roots in Shang society. Few, however, question the conclusion that the credit for systematization belongs to the Chou. Cf. also Tung Tso-pin, who has pointed out that Chou feudal titles do come from equivalent words in the Yin documents: Bulletin of the Academia Sinica, Vol. 6, No. 3, 1936.

4. For a general treatment of the long history of Chinese feudal institutions see Sjoquist, Karl O., Das Feng-chien-Wesen (der chinesische Feudalismus) nach Abhandlungen aus verschiedenen Dynastien, Berlin, Rudolph Pfau, 1938. See also Otto Franke, Geschichte des chinesischen Reiches, Vol. I, Berlin, 1930, pp. 133-150, for the traditional treatment of the rise of the feudal states in early Chou times.

5. Mei Ssu-p'ing 梅思平, "Ch'un-ch'iu Shih-tai-ti Cheng-chih Ho K'ung-tzu-ti Cheng-chih Ssu-hsiang," "春秋時代的政治和孔子的政治思想," Ku Shih Pien, 古史辨, Vol. II, 1930, pp. 162-163.

6. See the excellent treatment by Professor Derk Bodde in his China's First Unifier, Brill, Leiden, 1938; also his Statesman, Patriot, and General in Ancient China, New Haven, 1940.

7. A recent work by Dr. Tjan Tjoe Som 曾珠森 , Po Hu T'ung, 白虎通_, The Comprehensive Discussions in the White Tiger Hall, Vol. I, Leiden, Brill, 1949, gives an excellent account of the work of the Han scholars and the part they had in perpetuating the myth of ancient unity. The argument here is essentially that followed in the first two volumes of the Ku Shih Pien. See Note 11 below.

8. Bulletin of the Museum of Far Eastern Antiquities, No. 18, 1946, pp. 199-365.

9. Ibid, pp. 199-201.

10. See, for example, K. S. Latourette, The Chinese, their History and Culture, 3rd Edition Revised, New York, Macmillan, 1946, pp. 32-81, and C. P. Fitzgerald, China, a Short Cultural History, 3rd Edition Revised, New York, Praeger, 1950, Chapter III.

11. Volumes 1 through 7, 1926-1941. Volume 4 (1933) was edited by Lo Ken-tse 羅根澤. Ku discusses the con- clusions concerning the Chou period in his introduction to Volume 4, p. 5. Arthur W. Hummel reviewed the contents of Volume I for the American Historical Review, Vol. 34, 1929, pp. 715-724.

12. Chung-kuo ku-tai she-hui hsin yen ch'u-kao 中國 古代社會新研初稿, Peking, 1941.

13. Kuo Mo-jo's outstanding work for this period is his Chung-kuo Ku-tai She-hui Yen-chiu 中國古代社會研究, Researches in Ancient Chinese Society, 1929; see T'ao Hsi-sheng's Chung-kuo She-hui-chih Shih-ti Fen-hsi 中國社會之史的研究, An Analysis of the History of Chinese Society, Shanghai, 1929; Hou Wai-lu's Chung-kuo Ku-tai She-hui Shih 中國古代社會史, A History of Ancient Chinese Society, Shanghai, 1948, begins with the state- ment (p. 1), "In doing historical research, the first important task is to know the means of production of the period in question." Chi Chao-ting's Key Economic Areas in Chinese History, London, 1936, has been very favorably received both in China and in the West.

14. The historiography of the ":deep roots of Chinese Marxism" has been admirably documented by E. S. Kirby, op. cit. supra, Chapters II through VI.

15. On the burning of the books and especially the annals of the various courts see Edouard Chavannes' "Introduction" to his translation of the Mémoires historiques de Se-ma Ts'ien, Paris, Leroux, 1895, Vol. I, p. cliii, Note 1.

16. A good example of the point in question is the standard college textbook in China on Ancient Chinese History by Hsia Tseng-yu 夏曾佑, Chung-kuo Ku-tai Shih 中國古代史, Commercial Press, Shanghai, 1935. For the traditional history of the period this is an excellent text, but of 128 pages (34-162) devoted to the history of the Ch'un-ch'iu period 90 are devoted to the philosophers and their schools.

17. The number of states at the beginning of the Ch'un-ch'iu--i. e. 170--is based upon an examination of the early years of the classic text and the commentaries together with various other texts. It is the number commonly accepted by modern scholars. Cf. Li Tung-fang 黎東方, The Ch'un-ch'iu and Chan-kuo 春秋戰國篇 in the Complete Discussions of Chinese History series Chung-kuo Li-shih T'ung-lun 中國歷史通論, Chungking, Commercial Press, 1944, p. 65.

18. As reported by Mencius, Meng-tzu 孟子, III, ix, 8; Legge, The Chinese Classics, Vol. II, p. 677.

19. On the style of these commentaries and for samples see George A. Kennedy, "Interpretation of the Ch'un-ch'iu," Journal of the American Oriental Society, Volume 62, No. 1, pp. 40-48.

20. Creel, H. G., Confucius, The Man and the Myth, New York, John Day, 1949, p. 202. Professor Creel's recent work utilizes the writings of the modern Chinese historians and their new approach to the Ch'un-ch'iu period. His account of the forging of the rosy picture of antiquity, 189ff., is especially good.

21. See Bernhard Karlgren, "On the Authenticity and Nature of the Tso-chuan," Goteborgs Hogskolas Arsskrift, Vol. 32, No. 3, 1926, 65 pp; T'ang Hsiang-k'uei 湯向奎, "Lun Tso-chuan-chih Hsing-chih chi ch'i yü Kuo-yü-chih Kuan-hsi" 論左傳之性質及其與國語之關係, Shih-hsüeh Chi-k'an 史學季刊, No. 2, Oct. 1936, pp. 41-81; Lou Kan-jou, op. cit., pp. 25-30; and Professor William Hung's Introduction to the Concordances, Harvard-Yenching Sinological Index Series, Peking, 1937. This last lengthy discussion has been almost too enthusiastically summarized

in English by Ch'i Ssu-ho 齊思和 , "Professor Hung on
the Ch'un-ch'iu," <u>Yenching</u> <u>Journal</u> <u>of</u> <u>Social</u> <u>Studies</u>, Vol.
1, No. 1, 1938, pp. 49-71. The French sinologue Henri
Maspéro disagreed with Karlgren on several points. Following his review of Karlgren's work listed above
(<u>Journal</u> <u>asiatique</u>, vol. 212, 1928, pp. 159-165) Karlgren
elaborated "Early History of the Chou Li and Tso Chuan
Texts," <u>Bulletin</u> <u>of</u> <u>the</u> <u>Museum</u> <u>of</u> <u>Far</u> <u>Eastern</u> <u>Antiquities</u>,
No. 3, 1931, pp. 1-59. Maspéro's reply, "La composition
et la date du Tso Tchouan," <u>Mélanges</u> <u>chinois</u> <u>et</u> <u>bouddhiques</u>,
Vol. 1, 1931-1932, Brussels, 137-215, is a careful piece
of work representing the best tradition of the French
school of sinology. He breaks the <u>Tso-chuan</u> into three
component parts, the main one being the chronicle of the
struggle of the northern states against Ch'u.

22. Chavannes translated the first 47 of the 130
chapters of this magnificent Chinese history, <u>Les</u> <u>Mémoires</u>
<u>historiques</u> <u>de</u> <u>Se-ma</u> <u>Ts'ien</u>, (hereafter abb. <u>Mém</u> <u>hist</u>),
5 volumes, Paris, Leroux, 1895-1905. The Ch'in annals
constitute Chapter 5 of the <u>Shih-chi</u>; Chavannes, Vol. II,
pp. 1-99.

23. On the spurious vs. the authentic <u>Bamboo</u> <u>Annals</u>,
see Karlgren, "Legends and Cults," <u>loc.</u> <u>cit.</u>, p. 202. The
spurious edition is the one translated by James Legge,
<u>Chinese</u> <u>Classics</u>, Vol. III, Pt. I, "Prolegomena," pp. 108-
176. Henri Maspéro concluded that this "spurious" text
was genuine as a whole, "La Chronologie des rois de
Ts'i au IVe siècle avant notre ère," <u>T'oung</u> <u>Pao</u>, 25, pp.
367-386.

24. Lou Kan-jou, <u>op.</u> <u>cit.</u>, p. 25.

25. Karlgren, "Legends and Cults," pp. 201-202. It
is interesting that Professor Karlgren, who devotes some
167 pages to a discussion of what the Han historians did
to local legends and cults, should fail to see the political
side of the picture and its implications. See his statements quoted above. Nevertheless, his proposed method
of classification is an excellent one.

26. Roswell Britton, "Chinese Interstate Intercourse
before 700 B. C.," <u>American</u> <u>Journal</u> <u>of</u> <u>International</u> <u>Law</u>,
Vol. 29, 1935, p. 616.

27. The value of using such an approach is supported
by Harold D. Lasswell, <u>World</u> <u>Politics</u> <u>and</u> <u>Personal</u> <u>In-</u>
<u>security</u>, New York, Whittlesey House, 1935, pp. 3-9.
Professor Lasswell employs his "developmental analysis"

in surveying the problems of our modern world sovereign
state system.

28. Kennedy, op. cit. supra, note 19.

29. Tung Shu-yeh 童書業 , A History of the Ch'un-
ch'iu, Ch'un ch'iu Shih 春秋史 , Shanghai, Kaiming Book
Company, 1946. This work is by a student of Ku Chieh-
kang and is based upon lecture notes used by Ku. It is an
excellent summary of the most modern critical history
of the period and deserves to be translated into Western
languages.

30. Kennedy, op. cit., p. 45.

31. Mei Ssu-p'ing, op. cit., pp. 162-174.

32. Locating ancient Chinese cities and states is a
very difficult task and one on which Chinese geographers
have spent much effort. Our location of the cities involved,
in order to calculate distances, has been based upon the
following works: Ku Tung-kao 顧棟高 , Tables of Main
Events in The Ch'un-ch'iu, Ch'un-ch'iu Ta-shih Piao
春秋大事表 50 Chapters 卷 , Preface dated August 1748,
and the Ch'un-ch'iu Ta-shih Piao Yü-t'u, 春秋大事表興圖 ,
The Topography of the Main Events of the Ch'un-ch'iu,
Preface dated 1745, also by Ku. Both of these works
appear in the Huang-Ch'ing Ching Chieh Hsü-P'ien 皇清
經解續篇, Vol. 卌 17-34. Ku's work which is indispensible
to any student of the Ch'un-ch'iu is a systematic and
topical listing of events in various categories as given
in the Ch'un-ch'iu and Tso-chuan. Yang Shou-ching 楊
守敬 (q. v. Hummel, Eminent Chinese, p. 484), Ch'un-
ch'iu Lieh-kuo T'u 春秋列國圖, Maps of the Various
States of the Ch'un-ch'iu, Vol. II in his Li-tai Yu-ti T'u
歷代興地圖) Topographic Maps of All Ages, Preface dated
September 1906. 東洋讀史地圖 , Toyo Dokushi Chi Zu,
Historical Maps of Eastern Asia by 箭內互 Yanai Wataru,
published in Tokyo, 1931, Map. #2. Herrmann, Albert,
Historical and Commercial Atlas of China, Harvard-
Yenching Monograph Series No. 1, Cambridge, Mass.,
1935, pp. 14-15.

33. A good recent discussion of the increasing trade
and better economic life through the course of the Ch'un-
ch'iu is Li Tung-fang, op. cit., Chapter III, pp. 65-78. He
points up the constant progress in transportation and
communication.

34. Li Chien-nung 李劍農, "Hsien-Ch'in Huo-pi Chih-
tu Yen-chin K'ao" "A Study of the Progressive Change in

the Pre-Ch'in Currency System"先秦貨幣制度演進考 ,
in the She-hui K'e-hsüeh Chi-k'an 社會科學季刊, Social
Science Quarterly, Vol. 3, No. 3, March 1933, pp. 481-
510.

35. Tung Shu-yeh, op. cit., p. 236.

36. Legge, Chinese Classics, Vol. V, Pt. II, p. 538
and 542. Unless otherwise noted we shall use Legge's
translation of the Ch'un-ch'iu Tso-chuan with the exception of the transliterated names which will be changed to
the Wade-Giles system.

37. Tung Shu-yeh, op. cit., p. 235.

38. Legge, op. cit., p. 559 and p. 563. See also Lou
Kan-jou, op. cit., p. 97, and Wittfogel, "Foundations and
Stages," pp. 47ff. on the increasing prosperity and luxury.

39. Lou Kan-jou, pp. 97-99.

40. See, for example, John C. Ferguson's pamphlet,
The Four Bronze Vessels of the Marquis of Ch'i, Peking,
1928, 10 pp.

41. Lou Kan-jou, op. cit., p. 112.

42. Legge, pp. 797 and 799. On increased production
through the period see, Tung Shu-yeh, op. cit., pp. 235-
237, Lou Kan-jou, op. cit., pp. 81ff. A discussion of commercial development by the individual states is in Cheng
Hsing-hsün 鄭行巽 Chung-kuo Shang-yeh Shih 中國商業史 ,
A History of Chinese Commerce, Shanghai, Shih-chieh
Shu-chü 世界書局 , 1931, pp. 42-50.

43. Chi Chao-ting, op. cit., passim. Cf. also the
bibliography cited by E. S. Kirby, Introduction to the
Economic History of China, Chapters II-VI.

44. K. A. Wittfogel, Wirtschaft und Gesellschaft
Chinas, Leipzig, 1931.

45. Lou Kan-jou, op. cit., pp. 97-99. See also the
first part of Chien Po-tsan's 翦伯贊 article "Hsien-Ch'in
'Fa'-ti Ssu-hsiang chih Fa-chan"先秦 法的思想之發展 ,
"The development of Pre-Ch'in Legalist Thought," Chung-
kuo Fa-hsüeh Tsa-chih, 中國法學雜誌, New Series, Vol.
I, No. 1, September 1936, esp. pp. 59-61.

46. The modern scholar Ch'i Ssu-ho 齊思和 is one of
the foremost authorities on Chinese feudalism. See his
articles "Feng-chien Chih-tu yü Ju-chia Ssu-hsiang" 封建
制度與儒家思想 , "The Feudal System and Confucian
Thought," Yen-ching Hsüeh-pao 燕京學報, No. 22, Dec.
1938, pp. 175-223 and "A Comparison between Chinese
and European Feudalism," Yenching Journal of Social

Studies, Vol. IV, No. 1, Aug. 1938, pp. 1-15. His preoccupation with the formal aspects, however, prevents him
from seeing the gradual withering of the system even
before the Ch'un-ch'iu. He assigns to the Chan-kuo period
the credit for the breakup of feudalism.

Chapter III

1. Most of the traditional style histories give this
figure. For example, it is given by Ma Tuan-lin 馬端臨
in his treatment of feudalism in the Wen Hsien T'ung-k'ao
文獻通考 , Commercial Press, Shanghai, 1936, p. 2059b.
Cf. Li Ung Bing, Outlines of Chinese History, Shanghai,
Commercial Press, 1914, p. 23. This is a rather readable
history of China in English based completely upon uncritical tradition.

2. Ku Tung-kao, op. cit., Table 5, pp. 1a-15a, identifies 209 states which occur in the Ch'un-ch'iu and traces
their fortunes. Some of these states appear later in the
chronicle after the sphere of contact had enlarged, so the
figure given (170) is probably close. Cf. Ch'eng Te-hsu,
"International Law in Early China (1122-249 B. C.)",
Chinese Social and Political Science Review, Vol. 11,
1927, p. 42. Hou Wai-lu侯外廬 discusses the development
of the City-states of the Western Chou period in his
History of Ancient Chinese Society, Chung-kuo Ku-tai
She-hui Shih 中國古代社會史, Shanghai, 1948.

3. Ssu-ma Ch'ien lists 13 states, but calls them 12;
Chavannes, Vol. III, pp. 15-21 and 30-46. The discrepancy
has been accounted for in two possible ways: a. Wu
one of the states listed was not counted because of its
barbarian nature; b. Wu did not appear until 585 B. C.,
and by that time the term "12 rulers" was in common
usage, so Ssu-ma merely perpetuated it. Chavannes, III,
p. 15, Note 1. Note the different romanizations to distinguish between the States Wei衛 and Wey魏,and Hsü 許
and Sü徐.

4. Legge, Chinese Classics, V, p. 582 and 583. Unless
otherwise noted, references to Legge's works will be to
this edition of the Ch'un-ch'iu and Tso-chuan.

5. See Roswell Britton, "Chinese Interstate Intercourse
before 700 B. C. ", American Journal of International Law,
Vol. 29, 1935. This article, the first to direct modern

analytical techniques toward the analysis of the Ch'un-ch'iu, offered real inspiration for the present study. Britton analyzed the first twenty years of the chronicle as a "departure point for comparison with evolving custom in later centuries" (p. 635). He also was one of the first Western scholars to point to the fictional character of the Chou unity.

6. On this general characterization of the central states cf. Mei Ssu-p'ing, op. cit., pp. 162-3. He says, "by the Ch'un-ch'iu period the progress of these states was all but stopped. Since they were all enclosed in one territory, and this being the case the culture of the same degree, they therefore were equally unable to develop and on the governmental side they were unable to cast off the old remnants of feudalism." (p. 163); also Henri Maspéro, La chine antique, Vol. IV of the "Histoire du monde" series, Paris, Boccard, 1927, pp. 286-7.

7. The Chinese are perhaps the world's most enthusiastic genealogists. For a recent recreation of the genealogies of the various states see Sun Yao孫曜, Ch'un-ch'iu Shih-tai chih Shih-tsu春秋時代之世族 A Genealogy of the Ch'un-ch'iu, Shanghai, China Book Co., 1931. See also Ch'un-ch'iu Fen Chi春秋分記 Separate Records of the Ch'un-ch'iu by the Sung scholar Ch'eng Kung-t'ung 程公統 in the Commercial Press selections from the Ssu-k'u Ch'uan-shu 四庫全書 in 90 chapters. Book I, Chapters 1-18, gives the genealogical tables of rulers and ministers of the various states.

8. "Yen Wu Fei Chou Feng-kuo Shuo"無吳非周封國説 "That Yen and Wu were not states enfieffed by Chou", Yen-ching Hsueh-pao, No. 28, 1940, pp. 175-196. Lou Kan-jou, op. cit., p. 42, says, "We know then that these genealogical trees have no scientific basis at all, that in ancient China there were several peoples more or less independent from one another, that the Chou properly speaking played only a limited role under the dynasty which carried their name."

9. Ch'un-ch'iu Kuo-chi Kung-fa春秋國際公法, Shanghai, China Book Co., 1937. Chapter 1, pp. 1-9. A later work by Ch'en Shih-ts'ai is A Fragment on the Equality of States, an unpublished Harvard doctoral dissertation, 1945. Dr. Ch'en did publish some of his findings in the form of an article "The Equality of States in Ancient China," American Journal of International Law, Vol. 35,

1941, pp. 641-650. He discusses his proposition, however, with the assumption that the traditional Chou feudal system was in rigid operation.

10. Wolfram Eberhard, Lokalkulturen im alten China, Vol. I issued as a supplement to Vol. 37 of T'oung Pao, Leiden, Brill, 1942; Vol. II issued by the Catholic Press in China, Monumenta Serica Monograph Series No. 3, 1945. See also Eberhard's "Early Chinese Cultures and Their Development: a new working-hypothesis," Annual Report of the Smithsonian Institution, 1937, pp. 513-530.

11. Legge, Chinese Classics, Vol. V, I, p. 324.

12. Ibid, II, pp. 673 and 675.

13. Ibid, I, pp. 177-178 and 301-302. Ch'en Shih-ts'ai ignores these and many similar instances recorded in the Ch'un-ch'iu itself when he maintains that there was no peaceful intercourse with the barbarian states which were not considered equal, op. cit., p. 644.

14. Harvard-Yenching Concordances, Vol. I.

15. Legge, Chinese Classics, Vol. V, II, pp. 530 and 533.

16. The system of ranks and of ceremonies accompanying each rank is elaborately laid out in the Chou Li 周禮 or Rites of Chou a later work which attributed to the Chou dynasty all the formal organization which the Han scholars would have liked it to have. It has been translated by Edouard Biot, Le Tcheou-Li ou Rites du Tcheou, Paris, L'imprimerie nationale, 1851, 2 volumes. The charts of the land allotments, official position, etc., of these various feudal lords are given in Ma Tuan-lin, op. cit., pp. 2059a ff.

17. Legge, op. cit., p. 94.

18. Tschepe's four books appear in the series Variétés Sinologiques published by the Catholic Mission Press in Shanghai; Histoire du Royaume de Ou (1122-473 av. J.-C.), No. 10 of the series, 1896; Histoire du Royaume de Tch'ou (1122-223 av. J.-C.), No. 22, 1903; Histoire du Royaume de Ts'in 秦 (777-207 av. J.-C.), No. 27, 1909, and Histoire du Royaume de Tsin, No. 30, 1910.

19. Legge, op. cit., pp. 150-151.

20. Ku Tung-kao, op. cit., table No. 4; Li Tung-fang, op. cit., pp. 114-125.

21. Legge, op. cit., pp. 815 and 816.

22. Ku Tung-kao, op. cit., Table IV, pp. 4a-6a.

23. Legge, op. cit., pp. 377 and 379.

24. Ibid, pp. 545 and 549. The officer was Shu-hou
叔侯.

25. Ibid, pp. 511 and 516.

26. Ibid, p. 310, 598 B. C.

27. Ku Tung-kao, op. cit., Table 4, "Borders of the
Various States," pp. 7a-8a, lists the various increments
in Ch'i's territory and how they were brought about. Cf.
also Table 7, pp. 11a-32b, for a description of Ch'i's
capital city and various other towns and territories.

28. Legge, op. cit., pp. 143 and 145-146.

29. Ibid, pp. 165 and 169.

30. Li Hsüan-po, Chung-kuo Ku-tai She-hui Hsin Yen
Ch'u-kao 中國古代新研初稿 A First Draft of New
Researches in Ancient Chinese Society, Peking, 1941.
This work by a modern trained sociologist and anthropologist has been enthusiastically received as opening a new
era of research on ancient society in China. For a review
of this work see Yang K'un 楊楚, P'ing Chung-kuo Ku-tai
She-hui Hsin Yen Ch'u-kao 評中國古代新研初稿,
Scripta Sinica, No. 2, 1946, 117-134. A more recent recent review of the author's latest opinions can be found in
his article "Ancient Chinese Society and Modern Primitive
Societies" which has been translated into English and
appears in Philobiblon, No. 2, September 1946, pp. 4-25.

31. Maspéro, La chine antique, pp. 296 ff. and Tung
Shu-yeh, op. cit., pp. 147-155.

32. A translation of the Kuan-tzu by the English
sinologue F. S. Drake is in preparation. Most accounts
of the work in Western languages are based upon the book
Kuan-tzu and so are quite uncritical. Professor E. H.
Parker wrote a series of articles on him in the New China
Review, Vol. II, June 1920, pp. 248-266; Vol. III, February
1921, pp. 1-11 and December 1921, pp. 405-413, Vol. IV,
April 1922, pp. 77-87. The Belgian translator Charles de
Harlez translated the first three chapters of Kuan-tzu and
discussed his work, Journal Asiatique, 9th Series, Vol.
VII, pp. 26-99. A more recent and critical treatment can
be found in Hsiao Kung-ch'üan 蕭公權, A History of Chinese
Political Thought, Chung-kuo Cheng-chih Ssu-hsiang Shih,
中國政治思想史, Chungking, Commercial Press, 1945,
pp. 146-169. See also E. R. Hughes, "Political Idealists
and Realists in China of the Fourth and Third Centuries
B. C.," Journal of the Royal Asiatic Society, North China
Branch, Vol. 63, 1932, pp. 46-64.

33. In addition to many accounts in the <u>Tso-chuan</u>, Chapter 6 of the <u>Kuo-yü</u> is devoted completely to the words and works of Kuan-tzu and Duke Huan. Kuan-tzu appears in the <u>Analects</u> of Confucius and several other 'free' pre-Han works.

34. Tung Shu-yeh, <u>op</u>. <u>cit</u>., p. 150.

35. <u>Shih-chi</u> Chapter 62, <u>Ssu-pu Pei-yao</u> 四部備要 edition, ts'e 卅 16, pp. 1a-2b. This Chapter has been translated by Evan Morgan in his <u>Guide to Wenli Styles and Chinese Ideals</u>, London, Probsthain and Co., 1912, pp. 118-127. We follow Morgan's translation with the exception of the substitution of "Duke Huan" for "Duke of Huan", p. 124.

36. Legge, <u>op</u>. <u>cit</u>., pp. 246 and 248, discusses this organization. A complete list of officers of the various states can be found in the <u>Ch'un-ch'iu Fen-chi</u> of Ch'eng Kung-t'ung, Chapter 41 ff. This state organization was patterned on a smaller scale after the first Chou feudal order. The <u>Chou Li</u> 周禮 gives a complete list of the duties of officials with similar titles under the idealized Chou empire.

37. <u>Kuo-yü</u>, Chapter 6, <u>Ssu-pu Pei-yao</u> edition, pp. 4b-5b. The note by a Confucian scholar in this edition reads, "This was Kuan-tzu's system and not the Chou method." A stinging comment!

38. <u>Ibid</u>, p. 7a. Cf. the author's article "The Control System of the Chinese Government," <u>Far Eastern Quarterly</u>, Vol. VII, No. 1, 1947, pp. 1-22.

39. Tung Shu-yeh, <u>op</u>. <u>cit</u>., p. 152.

40. T'ao Hsi-sheng 陶希聖 , <u>Chung-kuo She-hui Shih</u> 中國社會史 , <u>A History of Chinese Society</u>, Wen-feng Shu-chü 文風書局 , Chungking, 1944, p. 47. In the southern State of Ch'u this official was known as the <u>Ling-yin</u> 令尹 .

41. <u>Op</u>. <u>cit</u>., p. 1b.

42. <u>Kuo yu</u>, <u>op</u>. <u>cit</u>., 8a; Maspéro, <u>La chine antique</u>, gives perhaps the best critical appraisal of Kuan-tzu's work in his treatment of the "Hegemony of Ch'i," pp. 281-313.

43. This term has been variously translated as 'hegemon,' 'tyrant,' or 'protector.' The last interpretation is to be preferred since, in fact, Duke Huan was the protector of the Chou states. He was the first of the famous Wu-pa 五霸 , or "Five Protectors", who at various times through the course of the Ch'un-ch'iu undertook the

protection of the central states and the House of Chou against the threat of subjugation by one of the other larger outer states.

44. Kuo-yü, op. cit., pp. 8a-10b.

45. A convenient table of the meetings is given by Li Tung-fang, op. cit., Chapter I, Note 49. Note 55 lists the 28 instances of military activity carried on by Duke Huan. (pp. 16-20).

46. "Revolutionary" is the term used by some authors. Cf. Mei Ssu-p'ing, op.cit., p. 164.

47. Ibid, p. 165. Cf. Liang Ch'i-ch'ao History of Chinese Political Thought during the early Tsin Period, London, Kegan Paul, 1930, Tr. by L. T. Chen, p. 24.

48. In 548 B. C., Legge, op. cit., pp. 513 and 517.

49. In 621 B. C., Ibid, pp. 242 and 243-244. This was apparently a reorganization which followed the rule of Duke Wen. His reforms are not discussed in detail.

50. In 543 B. C. (Ibid, pp. 553-554 and 558) this was the important set of reforms carried out by the famous minister of Cheng, Tzu-ch'an子產 .

51. In 594 B. C. (Ibid, pp. 327 and 329) Lu introduced a new tax on land levied by the central government; and in 483 B. C. a new regulation was passed requiring military contributions to the state by all the people, pp. 827 and 828.

52. See, for example, Ch'ien Po-tsan, op. cit., p. 60 and Mei Ssu-p'ing, op. cit., p. 179.

53. Legge, op. cit., pp. 554 and 558, 734.

54. Mei Ssu-p'ing, op. cit., pp. 164-169.

55. Tung Shu-yeh, op. cit., p. 272. Mei Ssu-p'ing, op. cit., p. 173, notes that by the closing years of the Ch'un-ch'iu the final steps from a feudal to a centralized system had been taken.

56. Karlgren, "On the Authenticity and Nature of the Tso-chuan," loc. cit., has demonstrated by modern linguistic methods the existence of different dialects, even in written style, at a date much later than the Ch'un-ch'iu. See also Wolfram Eberhard's works cited in Note 10 above. Karlgren's "Legends and Cults in Ancient China," loc. cit., adduces further evidences on localism and in addition is an excellent bibliographical source on this topic. A rather uncritical argument on the other side is presented by Evan Morgan in his article "A League of Nations in Ancient China," Journal of the North China

Branch of the Royal Asiatic Society, Vol. 62, 1926, pp.
50-56. In criticising former characterizations of the
league which was formed in 546 B. C., as a "League of
Nations' he states flatly that "in China the league was
formed of the same race and people having the same
language, descent, history and so on. It was a league
constituted of different parts of the same empire." (p. 51).
His argument is, of course, based upon the traditional
historical concept of Chou unity.

57. Hung Chun-p'ei, op. cit., p. 26.

58. Legge, op. cit., pp. 87 and 88.

59. Ibid, 542 B. C., pp. 559 and 563. On the cultural
autonomy of Ch'u see Lou Kan-jou, op. cit. , p. 63.

60. Ibid, pp. 369 and 371.

61. Ibid, pp. 205 and 210.

62. Ibid, pp. 786 and 787. See also pp. 350 and 352
for a statement of loyalty to Chin.

63. For example, Mencius (Meng-tzu孟子), Book I,
Part I; Legge, Chinese Classics, Vol. II, pp. 514 ff. Similar examples can be found in almost any other of the works
of the Chan-kuo. Cf. Lieh-tzu,列子 Ssu-pu Pei-yao edition, ts'e 册 2, pp. 11b-72a, where there is an account
of a man from Yen who rejoices to return to his home
state. Perhaps the best source on the patriotism of the
people in Ch'un-ch'iu times is the Shih-Ching 詩經 or
Book of Poetry. Many of its poems or songs are local in
origin and praise the local home territory. The section
called Kuo Feng國風 or "Airs of the States" contains
many expressions of loyalty to particular states. Thus,
for example, a princess who has been married to the
ruler of another state laments
            "My heart is in Wei
         There is not a day I do not think of it"
Legge, Chinese Classics, Vol. IV, Pt. I, Hongkong 1871,
p. 63. See also the "Praise Odes of Lu" esp. No. 4, probably written for Duke Hsi僖 , pp. 620-629.

64. For example in 520 B. C., when Chin calculates
its own interest first, and after it finds them in agreement
with the wishes of the Chou king, it makes a statement of
humble submission. Legge, op. cit., pp. 738-739 and 740.

65. Hung Chün-p'ei, op. cit., p. 39.

66. Legge, op. cit., pp. 269 and 271.

67. Lu was a regular attendant at the Chin court with
tribute. For a statement of how much this tribute was

valued see ibid, p. 549.

68. Ibid, p. 159.

69. Mencius, Legge, Chinese Classics, Vol. II, p. 250. For a discussion of the positions of these various types of states from a legal viewpoint see Ch'en Ku-yüan 陳顧遠, Traces of International Law in China, Chung-kuo Kuo-chi-fa Su-yüan, 中國國際法溯源, Shanghai, Commercial Press, 1934, pp. 19-39.

70. Legge, Chinese Classics, Vol. V, Part II, pp. 620 and 622.

71. Tung Shu-yeh, op. cit., p. 84.

72. Mencius was convinced that man's basic nature is good. His opponent Hsün-tzu (the counterpart of Hobbes in Western philosophy) believed man's nature to be bad and in need of restraint by law. Cf. Legge, Chinese Classics, Vol. II, "Prolegomena, " pp. 62-79 and 92-94.

73. Legge, Chinese Classics, Vol. V, Part I, pp. 365-366 and 367-368.

Chapter IV

1. Illustrations of some of these chariots are reproduced from the 六經圖考 Liu-ching T'u-k'ao (of the Southern Sung scholar Yang Chia 楊甲 by Hsü Chu'an-pao 徐傳保 in his Traces of International Law in Ancient China, Hsien-Ch'in Kuo-chi-fa chih Yi-chi 先秦國際之遺跡 , Shanghai, 1931, pp. 282-283. This work is an excellent collection of passages from 45 ancient texts, some free and some systematizing. The author makes no attempt to separate out the reliable texts, but the topical arrangement of the work makes it extremely valuable.

2. See Komai Kazuchika 駒井和愛 "An ancient bronze axlehead with a knife discovered in China," Toho Gakuho 東方學報, February 1936, No. 6, pp. 289-294 (with 5 illustrations).

3. On the military equipment see Tung Shu-yeh, op. cit., pp. 92 ff. There seems to be some disagreement as to who supplied the weapons for the men. Ch'i Ssu-ho, "A comparison between Chinese and European Feudal Institutions," loc. cit., p. 8, follows the accounts as given by Tso in assuming that the rulers rather than the men themselves supplied the weapons. Li Ung Bing, op. cit., p. 25, argues that the peasants supplied the weapons.

Both are probably right, and this would seem to be just another example of the error of attempts to find a uniform practice for all states under the assumed Chou "standards". An even better case in point is the attempt to reconcile the figures on the number of men who accompanied a chariot. On this point some commentators•have even ventured textual correction on the basis of assumed Chou standards. Cf. Tung Shu-yeh, op. cit., pp. 90-92. The different states used different schemes of army organization and were constantly changing and modifying them as new techniques developed.

4. The existence, let alone the increased use of iron, in the Ch'un-ch'iu, has been debated quite extensively by Chinese and Western scholars. The evidence seems to favor the affirmative side. See Hsü Chung-shu 徐中舒 , "耒耜考 " "Lei-sha k'ao," "On some Agricultural Implements of the Ancient Chinese," Bulletin of the Academia Sinica, Vol. II, Pt. I, 1930, pp. 11-59. Hsü's findings have been questioned by the English sinologist Arthur Waley, "Note on Iron and the Plough in Early China," Bulletin of the London School of Oriental Studies, Vol. XII, 3/4, 1948, pp. 803-804. Wu Ch'i-ch'ang 吳其昌 , "The History of Pre-Ch'in Agriculture in China," "秦以前中國田制史 ," "Ch'in Yi-ch'ien Chung-kuo T'ien-chih Shih," She-hui K'e-hsüeh Chi-k'an, 社會科學季刊 , Vol. 7, No. 3, July 1935, pp. 543-584 and No. 4, August 1935, pp. 833-872; Chu Hsi-tsu 朱希祖 "An examination of the antecedents in the south of ancient Chinese arms made of iron," "Chung-kuo Ku-tai T'ieh-chih Ping-p'in Hsien-hsing yü Nan-fang K'ao," "中國古代鐵製兵器先行於南方攷," Ch'ing-hua Hsüeh-pao 清華學報, Vol. V, No. 1, pp. 1475-1488; and Tung Shu-yeh, op. cit., p. 237 all assert the importance of iron by Ch'un-ch'iu times.

5. One of the best descriptions of the warfare of the Ch'un-ch'iu was compiled by the French sinologist Edouard Biot on the basis of the material furnished in the Shih Ching or Book of Poetry which Ku Chieh-Kang identifies as the only authentic pre-Chan-kuo text, (Ku-shih Pien, Vol. II, pp. 418-419), Journal Asiatique, 4th series, Vol. II, 1843, pp. 307 ff. and 430 ff. This has been translated into English by James Legge in his prolegomena to his translation of the Shih Ching, Chinese Classics, IV, I, pp. 142-171. See also H. G. Creel, The Birth of China, London, Jonathan Cape, 1936, pp. 141-157.

6. Legge, op. cit., p. 45.

7. Ibid, pp. 790 and 791.

8. Biot, op. cit.

9. Legge, op. cit., pp. 673 and 674.

10. There seems to be little doubt that canals had been constructed as early as the Ch'un-ch'iu period and that some were used for transporting troops. Bibliographical data on this score can be found in Chi Ch'ao-ting, Key Economic Areas in Chinese History, London, George Allen and Unwin, Ltd., 1936, pp. 50-57.

11. Legge, op. cit., pp. 160 and 161.

12. One fairly recent study is by Wan Kuo-ting 萬國鼎, "Han Yi-ch'ien Jen-k'ou chi T'u-ti Li-yung chih I-pan, "漢以前人口及土地利用之一斑," "Population and Land Utilization in China, 1400 B.C.-200 A.D." Chin-ling Hsüeh-pao 金陵學報, Vol. I, No. 1, May 1931, pp. 133-150.

13. T. Sacharoff, The Numerical Relations of the Population of China during the 4000 Years of its Historical Existence, translated from the Russian into English by Rev. W. Lobscheid, Hongkong, 1852, pp. 6-7.

14. Tung-Shu-yeh, op. cit., p. 92.

15. Mei Ssu-p'ing, op. cit., pp. 163-164 and Maspéro, op. cit., pp. 286-294.

16. Ch'i Ssu-ho, "A Comparison between Chinese and European Feudal Institutions," loc. cit., p. 4.

17. Legge, op. cit., pp. 135 and 136.

18. Ibid, p. 596.

19. As for example in 719 B.C., Ibid, pp. 15 and 16.

20. Ibid, p. 548.

21. Lou Kan-jou, op. cit., pp. 84-87. Tung Shu-yeh, op. cit., lists the implements which were developed and the main crops of the Ch'un-ch'iu period, pp. 49-53. See also Liu Ta-chün 劉大鈞, "Chung-Kuo Ku-tai T'ien-chih Yen Chiu,"中國古代田制研究, "Researches in Land Cultivation in Ancient China," Ch'ing-hua Hsüeh-pao, Vol. III, No. 1, June 1926, pp. 679-685.

22. Li Ung Bing, op. cit., p. 40.

23. Yen-tzu Ch'un-ch'iu,晏子春秋, Book V, No. 18 in the Yen-tzu Ch'un-ch'iu Chiao-chu,晏子春秋校注 edition of Chang Shun-yi 張純-Shanghai, World Book Co., April 1936, p. 137.

24. Lou Kan-jou, op. cit., pp. 311-315 and 316-319.

25. Legge, op. cit., pp. 696 and 699.

26. Ibid, pp. 767 and 769.

27. Ibid, pp. 391 and 396.

28. Ibid, pp. 15 and 16-17.

29. Ibid, In 569 B. C., pp. 421 and 423; and in 544 B. C., pp. 544 and 549.

30. Ibid, pp. 215 and 216-17.

31. Ibid, pp. 197 and 198-199.

32. Ibid, pp. 222 and 225.

33. Yen-tzu Ch'un-ch'iu, loc. cit., Book V, Chapter 17, p. 137.

34. Legge, op. cit., pp. 603 and 606.

35. Ibid, pp. 124 and 125.

36. Ibid, p. 159.

37. Ibid, pp. 444 and 448.

38. Ibid, pp. 774 and 777.

39. Ibid, 529 B. C., pp. 646 and 652.

40. Ibid, p. 105.

41. Ibid, pp. 646 and 652.

42. In the following interpretation of the Ch'un-ch'iu history as a balancing process focusing on Cheng as its center, the references are not given for the precise location of all events as recorded in the Ch'un-ch'iu and Tso-chuan. The analysis is based almost completely on these works, and the footnoting of every date would lead to an almost unbearable number of footnotes. For converting the dates given from the standard calendar of the West to the reign years of the dukes of Lu which in turn gives the location in the classic, cf. Mathias Tchang, Synchronismes Chinois, Variétés sinologiques No. 24, Shanghai, Catholic Mission Press, 1905, pp. 42-92. Hung Chün-p'ei, op. cit., pp. 111-117 discusses the position of Cheng and the many important contests which were waged for its control, but he does not refer to the events as a balancing process. Hung, pp. 117-121 also discusses the formation of leagues by the rival blocs of states. Professor Creel, who has probably examined the period as closely as any Western scholar, characterizes Cheng's position as "farcical," Confucius, loc. cit., p. 17; but consideration of Cheng's position as the center of a balancing process makes the many invasions which it suffered and its many changes of allegiance a bit more understandable. A brief but very vivid description of Cheng's peculiar position is given by Hellmut Wilhelm in his introduction to his translation of the works of Teng Hsi-tzu 鄧析子, "Schriften und Fragmente

zur Entwicklung der Staatsrechtlichen Theorie in der
Chou-Zeit," Monumenta Serica, XII, 1947, pp. 45-46.

43. Tung Shu-yeh, op. cit., p. 96, discusses Cheng's
strength and points out that it was never a weak state
despite the fact that it was hemmed in by powerful neighbors.

44. The rivalry between Ch'u and Chin has been extensively treated by Tschepe in his Histoire du royaume
de Tsin, loc. cit., pp. 130 ff. and 161 ff.

45. Legge, op. cit., pp. 433 and 435 where a Cheng
advisor says, "The army of Ch'u has come from far; its
provisions will soon be exhausted; it must shortly retire,"
and pp. 444 and 448 where it is pointed out that the armies
led by Chin cannot stay in Cheng for long.

46. It did, however, have some backing from Ch'u
at the time. Ibid, pp. 287 and 289.

47. Ibid, pp. 433 and 435.

48. Ibid, p. 147.

49. Mei Ssu-p'ing, op. cit., p. 165, points out that
there had been no revolts in Ch'in during the course of
the Ch'un-ch'iu.

50. On the story of Wu's rise to power and its policy
of alignment with Chin against Ch'u, cf. Tschepe, Histoire
du royaume de Ou, loc. cit.

51. Perhaps the reason why the history of the Ch'un-
ch'iu has not heretofore been analyzed in terms of the
balance of power process is that there are no writings
which have come down from the period in which the statesmen used such terminology. There was also the fact that
it was still a matter of opposition between the Chou states
and some outer "barbarians." In the later Chan-kuo period
there was not only a balancing process in operation but a
well developed theory of balance of power, part of which
has been transmitted. On this later development see
Peter Theunissen's dissertation Su Ts'in und die Politik
der Langs-und Quer-Achse im chinesischen Altertum,
Breslau, 1938.

52. Legge, op. cit., p. 596.

53. Ibid, pp. 733 and 734.

54. Ibid, pp. 657 and 659.

55. Ibid, pp. 340 and 346.

56. Ibid, pp. 386 and 388.

57. Ibid, pp. 386 and 388.

58. Tung Shu-yeh, op. cit., charts this increase very

clearly, pp. 94-98. Cf. also Legge, op. cit.

59. Ibid, pp. 418 and 419.

60. Many Chinese writers take the battle of Ch'eng-p'u in 632 B. C., as an important turning point in Ch'un-ch'iu history. This was the first great battle between the Chou league and the league of states to the south. There-after most of the engagements were on a much more ex-tensive scale. Mei Ssu-p'ing, op. cit., p. 162 and 168; Tung Shu-yeh, op. cit., pp. 179-180. An extensive account of the battle is given by Tschepe in his Histoire du royaume de Tsin, loc. cit., pp. 85 ff.

61. Op. cit., p. 168.

62. A very vivid and lengthy account of this confer-ence is given in the Tso-chuan, Legge, op. cit., pp. 528-531 and 532-535. The general disarmament movement and move for peace has been discussed by Tung Shu-yeh, op. cit., pp. 222 ff; Ch'en Ku-yuan, op. cit., pp. 189 ff; and Tschepe, Histoire du royaume de Tsin, loc. cit ., pp. 288 ff.

63. The general conference which was held in Sung in 546 B. C., has been quite thoroughly studied by Western Scholars. Immediately after the Treaty of Versailles, when the League of Nations was enjoying its initial popu-larity several articles were written about this conference, calling it the "First League of Nations." Among these were "The first League of Nations" by G. G. Warren, New China Review, I, August 1919, pp. 356-367 and "Le Congrés de la Paix en Chine en 546 avant J. -C.," Les Études, 5 July 1918, pp. 77-82. Evan Morgan criticized these accounts on the ground that the various political units of the Ch'un-ch'iu were not states, ("A League of Nations in Ancient China," Journal of the North China Branch of the Royal Asiatic Society, Vol. LVII, 1926, pp. 50-56) but actually this was probably the only part of the comparison which was accurate. The meetings of the states which followed the 546 conference were different from former meetings only in that certain of the northern states came to Ch'u and some of the southern states appeared at the Chin court. Mr. Morgan does suggest that a comparison with the Hague conference would probably have been more accurate.

64. Legge, op. cit., pp. 531 and 534.

Chapter V

1. Roswell Britton, op. cit., p. 617.
2. Cf. Liang Ch'i-ch'ao, op. cit., pp. 23-25.
3. Works of Marxist slant, devoted to analysis of the society of Ch'un-ch'iu times, are: Kuo Mo-jo 郭沫若 , Researches in Ancient Chinese Society, Chung-kuo Ku-tai She-hui Yen-chiu 中國古代社會研究 , Shanghai, 1931; Hou Wai-lu侯外廬 A History of Ancient Chinese Society, Chung-kuo Ku-tai She-hui Shih,中國古代社會史, Shang-hai, Hsin-chih Shu-tien 新知書店 , January 1948. Non-communist works of equal value are T'ao Hsi-sheng 陶希聖History of Chinese Society, Chung-kuo She-hui Shih,中國社會史 Chungking, Wen-feng Shu-chü, 文風 書局 , 1944 and Lou Kan-jou, Histoire sociale de l'époque Tcheou, loc. cit. ; the last work is a doctoral dissertation written in Paris under the guidance of Professors Paul Pelliot and Henri Maspéro.
4. Legge, op. cit., pp. 44 and 46.
5. Ibid, pp. 379 and 381.
6. For example, in the field of external affairs, which concerns us most, there was a shift away from personal rule to control by a specialized group of functionaries. Hung Chün-p'ei, op. cit., p. 216, lists nine different types of diplomatic officials who were carrying out external policies by the end of the Ch'un-ch'iu period.
7. Professor Creel, Confucius, loc. cit., p. 188, generalizes on the period as a whole: "There is a great deal of evidence. . . that important offices were commonly handed down in noble families", and goes on in a footnote to explain, "This is my conclusion on the basis of examination of the literature and inscriptions." (Note 10, p. 316) But the earlier Chinese students of the Ch'un-ch'iu period had already studied this aspect in great detail. Ku Tung-kao, op. cit., even gives the genealogies of the important families of ministers, Table XII.
8. Legge, op. cit., pp. 83 and 84.
9. Ibid, pp. 148 and 149.
10. Ibid, p. 371.
11. Ibid, pp. 738 and 741.
12. Tung Shu-yeh, op. cit., pp. 237 ff. Mei Ssu-p'ing, op. cit., p. 189.

13. Legge, op. cit., pp. 514-15 and 619.

14. On Huan's nature as a hero cf. James Legge, "Two Heroes of Chinese History," China Review, Vol. I, June 1873, pp. 370-377.

15. Mencius, Meng-tzu   , Book I, Part I, Chapter 7, Legge, Chinese Classics, Vol. II, p. 13.

16. Lü-shih Ch'un-ch'iu 呂氏春秋, Ssu-pu Pei-yao 四部備要 Edition, ts'e 册 1, Chapter 2, pp. 7b-10a. Cf. Marcel Granet, Danses et legendes de la Chine ancienne, Paris, Alcan, 1926, Vol. I, pp. 79-81.

17. Mei Ssu-p'ing, op. cit., p. 177.

18. The influence of the rich merchants reached its peak during Chan-kuo times when many of them became quite famous. Ssu-ma Ch'ien even devoted a chapter of his Shih-chi to some of them, Ch. 129.

19. According to the Ch'un-ch'iu and Tso-chuan, these marriage alliances could lead to friction and division just as often as they could lead to peace and power. The question frequently arose as to which son of which wife (there were many of them) would get the throne. Thus, for example, the fact that the son of the Ch'in wife was not put on the throne in Chin led to war between those two states in 620 B. C., Legge, op. cit., p. 248.

20. For example, in 660 B. C., the ruling family of Wei scattered to several states. Ibid, pp. 126-127 and 129.

21. Ibid, pp. 407 and 409.

22. Ibid, p. 410.

23. Chinese literature abounds with stories about this man. It is difficult to sort the legend from the fact. Our account here is based mainly upon that given in the Tso-chuan. James Legge has written somewhat extensively about him, "Two Heroes in Ancient Chinese History," China Review, Vol. I, June 1873, pp. 377-381. Maspéro, La Chine Antique, pp. 318 ff. discusses his work in making Chin the leading state. The stories in the Kuo-yü, Chapter (chüan 卷) 10, Ssu-pu Pei-yao Edition, pp. 1a-20a, are mostly shortened versions of those in the Tso-chuan. Ssu-ma Ch'ien also discusses him quite extensively, Chapter XV (Chavannes, Mém. hist., IV, pp. 294-308); his account is also derived mainly from the Tso-chuan. Stories about Duke Wen also appear in such works as Lieh-tzu 列子, Ssu-pu Pei-yao 四部備要 Edition, pp. 4b-5a

(translated by Richard Wilhelm, <u>Lia</u> <u>Dsi</u>, Jena, Diederichs, 1921, p. 96) and the <u>Lü</u>-<u>shih</u> <u>Ch'un</u>-<u>ch'iu</u> 呂氏春秋, <u>Ssu</u>-<u>pu</u> <u>Pei</u>-<u>yao</u> Edition, pp. 10a-10b (translated by Richard Wilhelm, <u>Frühling</u> <u>und</u> <u>Herbst</u> <u>des</u> <u>Lü</u> <u>Bu</u>-<u>We</u>, Jena, Diederichs, 1928, pp. 415-416). Tschepe, <u>Histoire</u> <u>du</u> <u>royaume</u> <u>de</u> <u>Tsin</u>, <u>loc.</u> <u>cit.</u>, pp. 59-65 and 70-98, gives an account of Duke Wen from the point of view of the state which he ruled. For a traditional account of the position of this great leader, see the <u>T'ung</u>-<u>chien</u> <u>Kang</u>-<u>mu</u> 通鑑綱目 edited by Chu Hsi 朱熹 in 1172 A. D. (translated by de Mailla, <u>Histoire</u> <u>générale</u> <u>de</u> <u>la</u> <u>Chine</u>, Paris, 1777, Vol. II, pp. 132-141).

24. Legge, <u>op.</u> <u>cit.</u>, pp. 184-185 and 186-187.
25. <u>Ibid.</u>
26. Mei Ssu-p'ing, <u>op.</u> <u>cit.</u>, p. 165.
27. Legge, <u>op.</u> <u>cit.</u>, pp. 185 and 187.
28. <u>Ibid</u>, pp. 537 and 541.
29. <u>Ibid</u>, pp. 574 and 581.
30. As in the case of Duke Wen of Chin, the stories about Tzu-ch'an, the famous statesman of Cheng, can be found in many free pre-Han texts. A recent <u>Critical</u> <u>Biography</u> <u>of</u> <u>Tzu</u>-<u>ch'an</u> by Cheng K'o-t'ang 鄭克堂, <u>Tzu</u>-<u>ch'an</u> <u>P'ing</u>-<u>chuan</u> 子產評傳, Commercial Press, Shanghai, 1941, deals with the stories from many sources and evaluates them in an attempt to build up a good picture. The best work in a Western language is "The Life of Tsze-ch'an 子產 " by E. R. Eichler, <u>China</u> <u>Review</u>, Vol. XV, 1886, pp. 12-23 and 65-78. Eichler attempts at least a rudimentary evaluation of the many Chinese works which he utilized. E. H. Parker's article on Tzu-ch'an, "What we may learn from Ancient Chinese Statesmen," <u>Asiatic</u> <u>Quarterly</u> <u>Review</u>, January 1909, pp. 100-130, does not approach the standards set by Eichler, nor does the treatment by the German sinologist Alfred Forke, <u>Geschichte</u> <u>der</u> <u>alten</u> <u>chinesischen</u> <u>Philosophie</u>, Hamburg, Friederichsen and Co., 1927, pp. 92-98. Cf. also Hellmut Wilhelm, "Schriften und Fragmente," <u>loc.</u> <u>cit.</u>, pp. 46 ff. In the older Chinese sources, the fullest account of Tzu-Ch'an is to be found in the <u>Tso</u>-<u>chuan</u>. His works are also discussed extensively by Ssu-ma Ch'ien in the <u>Shih</u>-<u>chi</u> 史記, Chapters 31, 40, 42, and 47 (Chavannes, <u>Mém.</u> <u>hist.</u> Vol. IV, pp. 13 and 480-482; Vol. V, pp. 337-8 and 359). Confucius makes many complimentary statements about Tzu-ch'an in the <u>Analects</u>, <u>Lun</u>-<u>yü</u> 論語 (Eg. V, 14; XIV, 9; and

XIV, 10; Legge, <u>Chinese Classics</u>, Vol. I, pp. 42 and 142).
A short biography is also included in the <u>Shih Chi</u>, Chapter
119, "Perfect Statesmen" cf. also the <u>Lü-shih Ch'un-ch'iu</u>
呂氏春秋, XV, XVI, and XXII (Wilhelm's translation pp.
216 ff. and 399) and <u>Lieh-tzu</u> 列子, VI, 4 and VII,-8
(Wilhelm's translation pp. 69 and 80-82).

    31. Ssu-ma Ch'ien, <u>Shih-chi</u> 史記, <u>Ssu-pu Pei-yao</u>
Edition, Chapter 119, pp. 2a-2b. On his death see also
Legge, <u>op. cit.</u>, pp. 680 and 684-685.

    32. <u>Lü-shih Ch'un-ch'iu</u>, <u>loc. cit.</u>, Chapter XXII,
pp. 15a-15b, (Wilhelm, <u>op. cit.</u>, p. 399).

    33. Legge, <u>op. cit.</u>, pp. 554 and 558.

    34. Hellmut Wilhelm, "Schriften und Fragmente,"
<u>loc. cit.</u>, p. 46.

    35. Legge, <u>op. cit.</u>, pp. 554 and 558.

    36. <u>Ibid</u>, pp. 554-555 and 558. Cf. <u>Lü-shih Ch'un-
ch'iu</u>, Chapter XVI, 5, R. Wilhelm, <u>op. cit.</u>, pp. 248-249.

    37. Legge, <u>op. cit.</u>, pp. 594 and 598.

    38. E. R. Eichler, "The Life of Tsze-ch'an 子產,"
<u>China Review</u>, Vol. XV, 1886, p. 16.

    39. <u>Ibid</u>, pp. 15-16.

    40. Legge, <u>op. cit.</u>, pp. 673 and 675. A carefully
worded note to Ch'in by Tzu-ch'an in 549 B. C., was in-
strumental in making lighter Ch'in's exactions as leader
of the Chou League. Eichler, <u>op. cit.</u>, p. 14.

    41. <u>Ibid</u>, p. 20.

    42. Shu Hsiang was also a rather famous statesman
of Ch'un-ch'iu times. He belonged to the second type
which we shall discuss below, and tried to maintain the
fiction of authority vested in the royal house. Tschepe,
<u>Histoire du royaume de Tsin</u>, <u>loc. cit.</u>, pp. 254 ff. , re-
ports extensively on his work in Chin. Cf. also Bodde's
translation of Feng Yu-lan's <u>History of Chinese Philosophy</u>,
Peking, Vetch, 1941, pp. 37 ff; Hu Shih 胡適, <u>A General
History of Chinese Philosophy</u>, <u>Chung-kuo Che-hsüeh
Shih Ta-kang</u>, 中國哲學史大綱 Shanghai, Commercial
Press, 1938, pp. 370 ff; <u>Lü-shih Ch'un-ch'iu</u>, <u>loc. cit.</u> ,
XXII, 5, R. Wilhelm, <u>op. cit.</u>, p. 339; and passages in the
<u>Tso-chuan</u>.

    43. Legge, <u>op. cit.</u>, pp. 607-608 and 609-610.

    44. <u>Op. cit.</u>, pp. 46-47. Incidentally, Shu Hsiang's
stand on this question did not last very long in his own
state of Chin which is recorded as casting its own laws
on tripods in 513 B. C., a little over two decades later.

45. Our main source on Yen-tzu is the work which bears his name, the Yen-tzu Ch'un- ch'iu 晏子春秋(abb. YTCC). On this work and its authenticity as a free pre-Han text, cf. the author's "Some Notes on the Yen-tzu Ch'un-ch'iu," Journal of the American Oriental Society, Vol. 73, 1953. References will be to the edition by Chang Shun-yi 張純一, Yen-tzu Ch'un-ch'iu Chiao-chu 晏子春秋 校注 , 2nd Edition, Shanghai, Shih-chieh Shu-chü 世界 書局 , April 1936.

46. YTCC, Chapter IV, Section 11, p. 106.

47. Ibid, Chapter VI, Section 16, pp. 165-166; Chapter V, Section 8, pp. 129-130.

48. Ibid, Chapter VI, Sections 16 and 17, pp. 165-166.

49. Eg., Ibid, Chapter V, Section 16, p. 136 where Confucius admires his ability as a diplomat.

50. Shih-chi 史記, Chapter 62, Ssu-pu Pei-yao Edition, pp. 1a-4b. Ssu-ma concludes his biography "If Yen-tzu were living, I would even be his chariot driver so much do I admire him." (p. 48).

51. Cf. Mei Ssu-p'ing, op. cit., p. 182 and also Woo Kang, Les trois théories politiques du Tchouen Tsieou, Paris, 1932. A more readable and a valuable account is H. G. Creel, Chinese Thought: From Confucius to Mao Tse-tung, Chicago, 1953, pp. 10-45.

52. YTCC, Chapter V, Section 2, pp. 123-124; Chapter III, Sections 1 and 2, pp. 67-69.

53. Legge, op. cit., p. 514.

54. Ibid, p. 248, see note 19 supra.

55. Ibid, pp. 767 and 769.

Chapter VI

1. For a brief description of these three works in English, cf. Latourette, op. cit., pp. 65 ff. and 776 ff. On the authenticity of the works, a matter which occupied many Chinese and western scholars, see the works cited by Dr. Charles S. Gardner in his Chinese Traditional Historiography, Cambridge, Harvard University Press, 1938, pp. 56-57, Note 69.

2. Probably the first person to compare the rules of interstate relations in Ch'un-ch'iu times to the modern law of nations was the American sinologist William A. P. Martin, who read a paper entitled "Traces of International

Law in Ancient China," before the International Congress
of Orientalists in Berlin in 1881 (Verhandlungen des 5
internationalen orientalisten Congresses, Berlin, 1881,
Part II, pp. 71-78). This paper reappeared in many
languages in many lands. It was published under the title
"Traces of International Law in China," in the International
Review, New York, 1883, pp. 63-77; reprinted in Paris
under the title "Les vestiges d'un droit international dans
l'ancienne Chine" in the Revue de droit international et de
legislation comparée, Vol. XIV, 1882, pp. 227-242; summarized by the Comte de Noidans under the title "Le droit
international dans l'ancien empire chinois," Revue de
Belgique, Vol. XLVII, 15 July 1884, pp. 308-313; and reprinted by Martin in his Lore of Cathay, London, 1901.
A Chinese version appeared in China in 1884 under Martin's
Chinese name Ting Wei-liang 丁韙良 and is preserved in
the collection entitled Hsi-cheng Ts'ung-shu 西政叢書,
Vol. 7, 1897, under the title Chung-kuo Ku-shih Kung fa
中國古世公法. Martin's study was short and merely
pointed out a few areas where there seemed to be quite
as much of a rudimentary interstate law in ancient China
as Western scholars had attributed to ancient Greece and
Rome. But as Roswell Britton has observed (op. cit., p.
618), "In regard to the early Chinese interstate situation
he, like others after him, accepted the conventional
Golden Age of the early Chou, and regarded the states
as 'fragments of a disintegrated empire.' " Most of the
allusions to an interstate law in Ancient China to be found
in Western works stem from this work by Martin. With
one notable exception, the rest of the work on the interstate law of the Ch'un-ch'iu (and Chan-kuo) has been done
by Chinese scholars who have been struck by the analogies
to be drawn between a period about which their traditional
education had given them a great store of information and
the international law which they have studied in the West.
The first Chinese to make an extensive study, following
up the provocative ideas of Martin was the careful scholar
Chang Hsin-cheng 長心徵 who published a 360 page book
entitled Interstate Law of the Ch'un-ch'iu Period, Ch'un-
ch'iu Kuo-chi Kung-fa 春秋國際公法, Peking, 1924. Five
years later Hsü Ch'uan-pao 徐傳保 conceived an even
more thorough method for studying the subject. He divided
his sources into those which reported on the facts about
the interstate law in Ancient China and those whose authors

theorized on the subject. One part, Les Idées, he published in French as a doctoral dissertation under the
title Le droit des gens et la chine antique, Paris 1926
(the French romanization for his name is Siu Tchoan-
pao); the other part, Les faits, was published in Chinese
in a large 658 page quarto volume, Shanghai, 1931, under
the title Traces of International Law in Ancient China
Hsien-Ch'in Kuo-chi-fa-chih Yi-chi 先秦國際法之遺跡 .
This latter work is the one the value and shortcomings of
which we have discussed above in the notes. In 1927, an
uncritical summary entitled "International Law in Early
China," was published by Ch'eng Te-hsü 程德諤 in the
Chinese Social and Political Science Review, Vol. XI, pp.
38-55 and 251-270. Not only are the dates converted into
the Western calendar incorrectly by Ch'eng, but he uses
as his main sources such works as the Tung-Chou Lieh-
kuo Chih 東周列國志, a novel about Eastern Chou times.
The next important study was a work by Ch'en Ku-yüan
陳顧遠 entitled Traces of International Law in China,
Chung-kuo Kuo-chi-fa Su-yüan 中國國際法溯源, Shanghai,
Commercial Press, 1934. Ch'en was the first Chinese to
stick fairly closely to the more reliable sources. This
work was followed by an even more critical work which
utilized all the works which we have listed so far, and
others which we have not listed because they have not
been available for our use: Hung Chün-p'ei 洪鈞培, The
Interstate Public Law of the Ch'un-ch'iu, Ch'un-ch'iu
Kuo-chi Kung-fa 春秋國際公法 , Shanghai, China Book
Co., Chung-hua Shu-chü 中華書局 , 1937. The latest of
these studies by Chinese students is an unpublished
doctoral thesis by Ch'en Shih-ts'ai, A Fragment on the
Equality of States, Harvard 1940. Dr. Ch'en did publish
his main argument as an article, "The Equality of States
in Ancient China," American Journal of International Law,
Vol. XXXV, 1941, pp. 641-650. Despite the fact that he
uses all the formal language of the modern international
lawyers, however, Dr. Ch'en's work follows the traditional interpretation of Ch'un-ch'iu history. He draws
heavily upon the Kung-yang and Ku-liang commentaries
to the Ch'un-ch'iu and insists that the rules for equality
which he adduces were applicable only to the Chou states.
The exception referred to above in the note is the study
of "Chinese Interstate Intercourse before 700 B.C.,"
American Journal of International Law, Vol. XXIX, 1935,

pp. 616-635, by Roswell Britton. This short work is by all odds the most scholarly of these works listed. Britton is extremely careful in his use of sources, makes no unwarranted generalizations, and is well up to date on the latest critical history of Ancient China.

3. Britton, op. cit., limits himself to these sources.

4. Hung, op. cit., p. 118; cf. also his Chapter V "Sources of the Interstate Law of the Ch'un-ch'iu," pp. 58 ff.

5. Ch'en Shih-ts'ai, "The Equality of States in Ancient China," loc. cit., p. 643.

6. Legge, op. cit., pp. 202 and 207.

7. Cf. Ch'en Shih-ts'ai, op. cit. Ch'en limits his argument to the Lieh-kuo 列國 but it is equally applicable to the other states.

8. Hung Chün-p'ei, op. cit., pp. 28 and 167-192; Ch'eng Te-hsü, op. cit., pp. 41-42.

9. On the foreign affairs officials see Ch'en Ku-yüan op. cit., pp. 91-94.

10. Legge, op. cit., pp. 744 and 753.

11. On this trend see a very careful and interesting article by Ch'i Ssu-ho 齊思和 "Chan-kuo Tsai-hsiang Piao 戰國宰相表" "Prime Ministers of the Warring States: A table with an introduction and two notes," Annual of History Shih-hsüeh Nien-pao 史學年表 , Vol. II, No. 5, December 1938, pp. 165-193--esp. p. 167.

12. The I-Li, translated by John Steele, London, Probsthain and Co., 1917, Vol. I, pp. 189-242 and 282-287.

13. Cf., for example, Legge, op. cit., pp. 238 and 239, where the ruler of Lu gives a banquet for a Wei envoy.

14. HsüCh'uan-pao, Hsien-Ch'in Kuo-chi-fa chih Yi-chih 先秦國際法之遺跡 , pp. 171-184 gives descriptions and diagrams of some of these buildings. They are, however, mostly gathered from traditional later sources.

15. YTCC, Chapter V, Section 16, pp. 135-137. This incident must have taken place between 547 and 532 B. C. since the reign of Duke P'ing of Chin covered the years 557-532 B. C. and that of Duke Ching of Ch'i 547-490 B. C.

16. Most of the works on interstate law listed in Note 2 discuss the rules governing the conduct of the diplomatic representatives. A good example of the important place of the Odes in diplomacy is given by Tso

for the year 544 B. C., Legge, op. cit., pp. 545-546 and
549-550.

17. Britton, op. cit., p. 624, observes that even during the first twenty years of the Ch'un-ch'iu "intercourse
was so frequent between some states as to amount to
constant communication virtually serving the purposes
of resident embassies."

18. On several occasions Tso reports on an envoy
encountering another envoy from his state at another
court.

19. Legge, op. cit., pp. 208 ff.

20. Ibid, p. 798.

21. Li Tung-fang 黎東方, op. cit., Note 49, pp. 16-
17.

22. Legge, op. cit., pp. 113 and 114.

23. HsüCh'uan-pao, op. cit., pp. 218 ff.

24. Legge, op. cit., pp. 117 and 118; 257 and 258.
For a detailed and highly imaginary account of the first
incident see Ts'ai Yüan-fang 蔡元放 ed., Tung-chou Lieh-
kuo Chih, 東周列國志, Chapter (hui 回) 21, 1792 Edition.

25. Legge, op. cit., pp. 434 and 436.

26. Ibid, pp. 362 and 364.

27. Ibid, pp. 585 and 588.

28. Ibid, pp. 429 and 431.

29. On this and the other types of documents (ceremonial records, li-chi 禮籍, credentials, chieh   ,
tablets of investiture, shui 瑞, etc.) see Hsü Ch'uan-pao,
op. cit., pp. 147-170.

30. Legge, op. cit., pp. 277 and 278.

31. Ibid, pp. 379-381 and 382-383.

32. In addition to the sections on treaties (usually
discussed under the modern term t'iao-yüeh 條約 though
that term is not used in the early sources) in the works
listed in Note 2, cf. also Shih Chao-ying 時昭瀛 "Treaties
in the Spring and Autumn Period" "Ch'un-ch'iu Shih-tai-
ti T'iao-yüeh 春秋時代的條約," in the Quarterly Journal
of Social Science, She-hui K'e-hsüeh Chi-k'an 社會科學
季刊, Vol. XI, No. 1, March 1931, pp. 20-37.

33. Li Ung Bing, op. cit., p. 15, gives an account of
these ceremonies, in English. Descriptions, based upon
the traditional interpretation of the Chou period, are
given in the three rituals. Of the works on interstate law
in the Ch'un-ch'iu cf., for example, Ch'en Ku-yüan, op.
cit., pp. 149-156.

34. Shih Chao-ying, op. cit., p. 20.

35. Roswell Britton, op. cit., pp. 626-628 analyzes the 16 meng recorded before 700 B. C. by the Ch'un-ch'iu. 9 were treaties of peace, 4 treaties of amity, 2 military pacts, and 1 a ratification of an exchange of territory. Of the 9 peace treaties, 7 were bipartite and 2 tripartite.

36. Legge, op. cit., pp. 377 and 378. We have rearranged the English translation of Legge and supplied numbers for the provisions in the same manner as that suggested by Hsü Ch'uan-pao, op. cit. for the treaty texts which he gives.

37. Legge, op. cit., pp. 379 and 381.

38. Ibid, pp. 386 and 388.

39. Ibid, pp. 351 and 353.

40. Ibid, pp. 316 and 321.

41. Ibid, pp. 205 and 211.

42. Ibid, pp. 214 and 215.

43. Hung Chün-p'ei, op. cit., pp. 139-140; Legge, op. cit., pp. 450 and 453.

44. Ibid, pp. 454 and 455.

45. Cf. Shih Chao-ying, op. cit., pp. 35-36 on the importance of these treaty oaths. On the enforcement of treaties, see also Hung Chün-p'ei, op. cit., pp. 233-238.

46. Legge, op. cit., pp. 415 and 417.

47. Ibid, p. 172 and Shih Chao-ying, op. cit., p. 35, cf. Yang Lien-sheng, "Hostages in Chinese History," Harvard Journal of Asiatic Studies, Vol. 15, Nos. 3/4, December 1952, pp. 507-521. Professor Yang lists three types of hostages: (1) exchanged, (2) unilateral, and (3) internal.

48. Chao Ch'ih-tzu 趙尺子, A History of Satellite States, Yin-kuo Shih 因國史, Taipei, Taiwan, January 1952, p. 5. Chao discusses twenty-seven of these cases in detail, Chapter VIII.

49. Ibid, pp. 36-37.

50. On the pacific settlement of interstate disputes, cf., for example, Ch'en Ku-yüan, op. cit., pp. 109-117. Ch'en's discussion of the position of the hegemon as a court of appeal in disputes is good.

51. Legge, op. cit., pp. 354 and 355.

52. Ibid, pp. 356 and 357.

53. Ibid, pp. 695-696 and 698.

54. Ibid, pp. 232 and 233.

55. Ibid, pp. 235 and 236.

56. Ibid, pp. 189 and 192.
57. Ibid, pp. 295 and 296.
58. Ibid, pp. 421 and 423; 545 and 549.
59. Ibid, pp. 545 and 549.
60. Britton, op. cit., pp. 630-632.
61. Legge, op. cit., pp. 803-804 and 804-805.
62. On these interstate conferences and their important part in developing commerce, see Lou Kan-jou, op. cit., pp. 100 ff. For a good general discussion of the meetings see Ch'en Ku-yüan, op. cit., pp. 184-212.
63. For example, the covenant signed in 631 B. C., Legge, op. cit., p. 215.
64. A most exhaustive study on the leagues, the functions which they served, their organization, and the rules connected with them is given by Hung Chün-p'ei, op. cit., Chapter II, pp. 109-150.
65. Britton, op. cit., p. 631.
66. Legge, op. cit., pp. 601-602 and 605.
67. Ibid, pp. 375 and 376; 695 and 697.
68. Ibid, pp. 485; 719 and 721.
69. Ibid, pp. 415 and 416.
70. Ibid, p. 97.
71. Ibid, pp. 222 and 225.
72. Ibid, pp. 369 and 371.
73. Ibid, p. 353.
74. Ibid, pp. 425 and 427.
75. Ibid, pp. 263 and 264.

Chapter VII

1. Hung Chün-p'ei, op. cit., pp. 18-24.
2. Bertrand de Jouvenel, On Power, New York, Viking Press, 1949, pp. 126-127.
3. See K. A. Wittfogel, "Foundations and Stages," loc. cit. supra.
4. Fung Yu-lan, History of Chinese Philosophy, tr. by Derk Bodde, 2nd edition, Princeton, Princeton University Press, 1952, p. 312.
5. Ch'i Ssu-ho, "Chinese and European Feudal Institutions," loc. cit., p. 2.
6. J. J. L. Duyvendak, The Book of Lord Shang, London, Probsthain, 1928.